CW00518620

The Romanov Legacy

The Romanov Legacy

The Palaces of St Petersburg

Zoia Belyakova

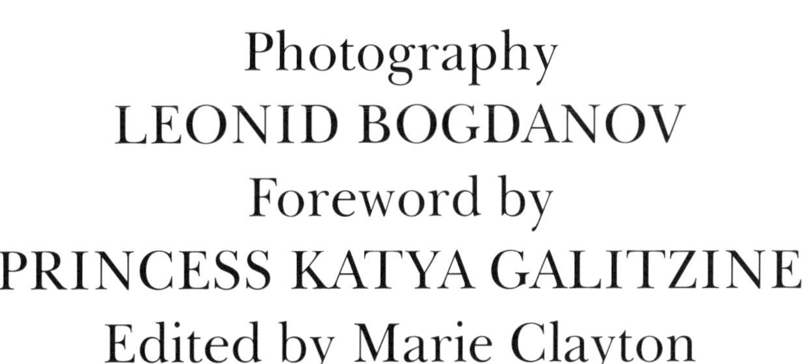

Photography
LEONID BOGDANOV
Foreword by
PRINCESS KATYA GALITZINE
Edited by Marie Clayton

HAZAR
PUBLISHING

Published in 1994 by Hazar Publishing Ltd
147 Chiswick High Road, London W4 2DT

A catalogue record of this title is available from the British Library

ISBN 1- 874371-27-X

Foreword by Princess Katya Galitzine

Edited by Marie Clayton

Designed by Robert Mathias, Publishing Workshop

Colour Separation by J Film Process, Singapore
Printed and bound by New Interlitho Italia Spa. Italy

Contents

FOREWORD

IN 1919 MY FATHER AND HIS FAMILY escaped from their homeland: Imperial Russia was disintegrating, their lives were threatened and the rule of Communism had begun. He was 3 years old. In 1989 I returned to St Petersburg to watch the epoch collapse, one of my father's last memories of Russia was to see the Soviet flag replaced by the pre-revolutionary tricolour. He was to die 3 years later. A full circle had passed, from his birth in old Russia to the burial of his ashes at the family home of Oranienbaum.

My father instilled in me great love and respect for the Russian people and a great pride in our history. Prior to living in St Petersburg, my knowledge of Russia was limited to black and white formal portraits of great grandparents, great aunts and other relatives and it was difficult to feel any personal connection to them. I never met my grandparents, but read about their lives at the Russian court in private journals and letters. My grandmother, Katya (I was named after her and all preceding grandmothers in that line) was one of the wealthiest heiresses in St Petersburg, belonging to the family Mecklenburg-Strelitz. They were direct descendants of Catherine the Great through her youngest grandson, Grand Duke Michael, son of Paul I. My grandfather, Prince Vladimir Galitzine, was a dashing young officer in the cavalier-guards and he eventually became aide-de-camp to the Grand Duke Nicholas Nikolayevich in the Caucasus. Our family name is one of the oldest in Russian history, so the match with Katya was approved by the Imperial court and they married in 1913. They drove in an automobile – a wedding gift – to their honeymoon at Oranienbaum where they spent most of the 10 days in the "chintz cosiness of the old nursery" (according to one letter to her sister) instead of the state apartments which had been specially prepared for them.

It was a time of greatest affluence in Russia, the aristocracy were still unaware of what was to take place in 1917. The ceremony of the Court, attending balls in palaces, feasting at grand banquets – all this was very much a part of my grandparent's lives. My grandfather, very good-looking in his white cavalier-guards uniform; my grandmother, as the eldest daughter, resplendent in the family jewels.

LEFT: The 'Triumph of Mars' by Giambattista Tiepolo, which was commissioned by the Russian Court for the ceiling in the Great Hall of the Chinese Palace. This painting was removed for safekeeping before World War II and then vanished.

GENEALOGICAL TABLE OF THE ROMANOVS

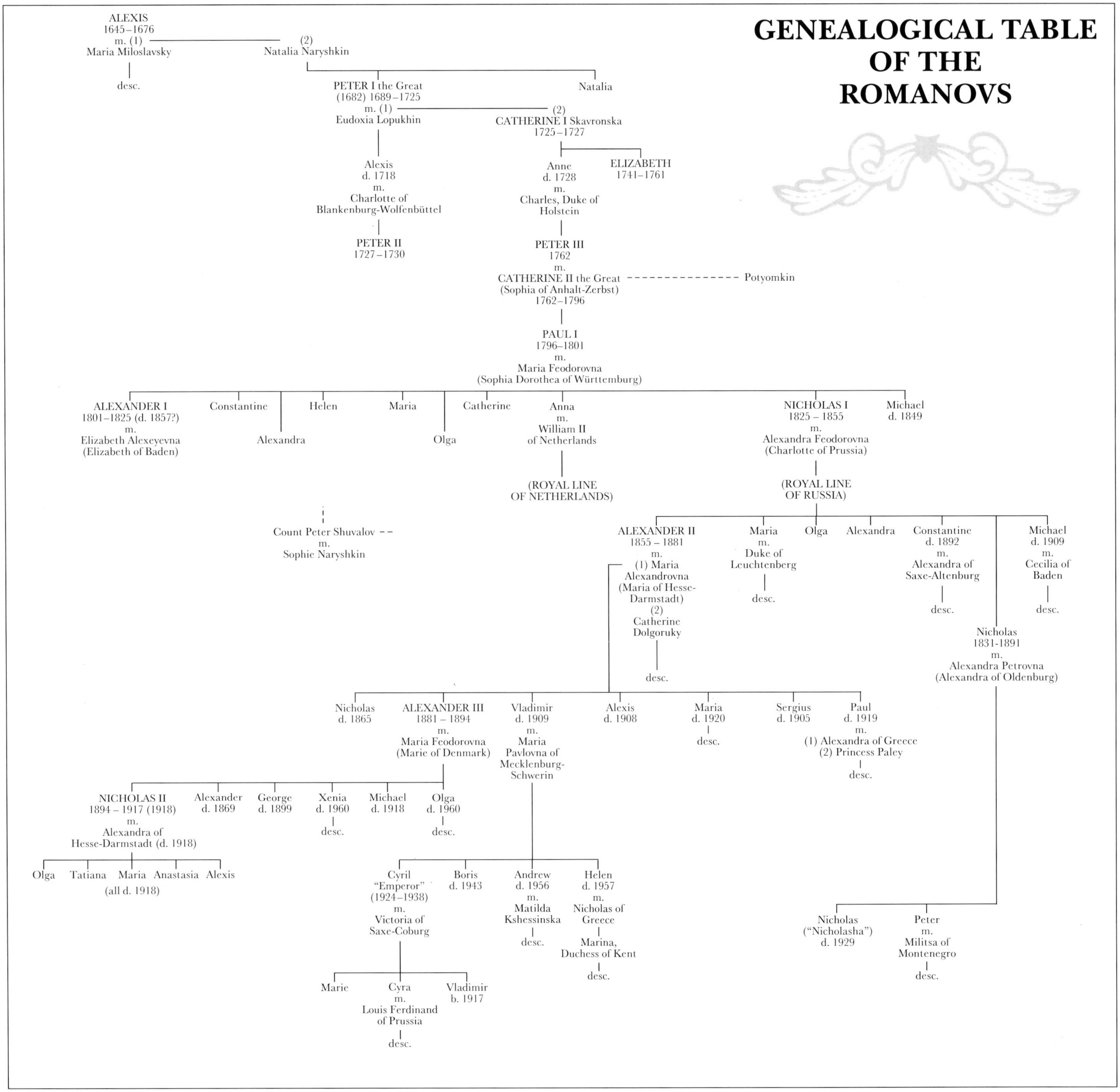

ALEXIS
1645–1676
m. (1)
Maria Miloslavsky
desc.

(2)
Natalia Naryshkin

PETER I the Great
(1682) 1689–1725
m. (1)
Eudoxia Lopukhin

Natalia

(2)
CATHERINE I Skavronska
1725–1727

Alexis
d. 1718
m.
Charlotte of
Blankenburg-Wolfenbüttel

PETER II
1727–1730

Anne
d. 1728
m.
Charles, Duke of
Holstein

ELIZABETH
1741–1761

PETER III
1762
m.
CATHERINE II the Great - - - - - - - - - - - - - - Potyomkin
(Sophia of Anhalt-Zerbst)
1762–1796

PAUL I
1796–1801
m.
Maria Feodorovna
(Sophia Dorothea of Württemburg)

ALEXANDER I
1801–1825 (d. 1857?)
m.
Elizabeth Alexeyevna
(Elizabeth of Baden)

Constantine

Alexandra

Helen

Maria

Olga

Catherine

Anna
m.
William II
of Netherlands
(ROYAL LINE
OF NETHERLANDS)

NICHOLAS I
1825 – 1855
m.
Alexandra Feodorovna
(Charlotte of Prussia)
(ROYAL LINE
OF RUSSIA)

Michael
d. 1849

Count Peter Shuvalov - -
m.
Sophie Naryshkin

ALEXANDER II
1855 – 1881
m.
(1) Maria
Alexandrovna
(Maria of Hesse-
Darmstadt)
(2)
Catherine
Dolgoruky
desc.

Maria
m.
Duke of
Leuchtenberg
desc.

Olga

Alexandra

Constantine
d. 1892
m.
Alexandra of
Saxe-Altenburg
desc.

Michael
d. 1909
m.
Cecilia of
Baden
desc.

Nicholas
1831-1891
m.
Alexandra Petrovna
(Alexandra of Oldenburg)

Nicholas
d. 1865

ALEXANDER III
1881 – 1894
m.
Maria Feodorovna
(Marie of Denmark)

Vladimir
d. 1909
m.
Maria
Pavlovna of
Mecklenburg-
Schwerin

Alexis
d. 1908

Maria
d. 1920
desc.

Sergius
d. 1905

Paul
d. 1919
m.
(1) Alexandra of Greece
(2) Princess Paley
desc.

NICHOLAS II
1894 – 1917 (1918)
m.
Alexandra of
Hesse-Darmstadt (d. 1918)

Alexander
d. 1869

George
d. 1899

Xenia
d. 1960
desc.

Michael
d. 1918

Olga
d. 1960
desc.

Olga Tatiana Maria Anastasia Alexis
(all d. 1918)

Cyril
"Emperor"
(1924–1938)
m.
Victoria of
Saxe-Coburg

Boris
d. 1943

Andrew
d. 1956
m.
Matilda
Kshessinska
desc.

Helen
d. 1957
m.
Nicholas of
Greece
Marina,
Duchess of Kent
desc.

Nicholas
("Nicholasha")
d. 1929

Peter
m.
Militsa of
Montenegro
desc.

Marie

Cyra
m.
Louis Ferdinand
of Prussia
desc.

Vladimir
b. 1917

My great-aunt, Tasha, wrote a romantic diary in the summer of 1912, which we still have in the family. She is a young 17 year old excited at the prospect of her first ball. "I would like so much to danse much! It is not that I would like to have success, but I'd like simply to danse." (English being the third language used, her spelling is sometimes not entirely correct) She, no doubt, had seen the polished wood floors of the palatial ballrooms and watched with envy her older sisters prepare for their 'danse'. She was to die the following year of infectious pneumonia, having attended only one ball. The park of Oranienbaum is described as "a dream; all the snow and the sunsets, the icy ponds. We have been driving in sledges and the woods are simply lovely. When it's sunny and it all glitters, it looks like Katya's eyes when she smiles, they glitter too, but they stay sad. I have never loved anything more than the glittery-sad smile of our woods." Her words are still true today. The park of Oranienbaum is one of the most enjoyable public spaces with boats on its upper and lower lakes, endless woods with sunlit clearings in summer, mushrooms and berries in autumn and a choice of hills for sledging in winter.

Hidden in the park is the exquisite Chinese Palace, each room with very much its own style and atmosphere. I think what adds to its beauty is the lack of artificial lighting, therefore one is dependent on the original lights of old: the sun streaming in through the French windows, the northern sunsets which match the pale cream and pink of the exterior walls. It is not surprising that UNESCO has protected it as one of the architectural wonders of the world. Yevgeniy Zamyatin wrote his futuristic novel "We" in the 1920s, in it the hero and his lover fly away from their rigid skyscraper life to a preserved palace in a park. It is supposedly situated in another region untouched by the modern authoritarian state in the book – I am not sure if Zamyatin knew of the Chinese Palace, but the surrounding park and lavish interior coincide with his described hideout. Possibly his imagination was influenced by the reality of Catherine meeting her lover, Grigory Orlov, in secret in this, her own "private dacha".

My grandmother Katya had great affection for her home at Oranienbaum, so full of historic interest and family associations. It was full of happiness for her, but on one occasion she had a terrifying vision: she saw the hall and familiar corridors full of an angry and menacing crowd with sticks and weapons forcing their way along. This was a very clear memory all her life.

A very clear memory for me is the first time I saw Oranienbaum. Nothing had prepared me for its vastness. And more shocking than its size was the terrible state of dilapidation, after being used as naval offices for so long. I was totally surprised by Katalnaya Gorka (the Switchback Pavilion), rising out of the spring snow like a 3-tiered celebration cake and fell in love with it immediately. I later found out that it was during my grandmother's childhood that the switchback itself was dismantled, her grandfather fearing for its safety. The children were never allowed into the Chinese Palace due to a crusty old great-aunt, who was feared by all the Imperial court. Even Grand Dukes were banished from her private concerts if they so much as coughed during a recital. These were my images of St Petersburg, the perfect setting for the fairy-tales of Tchaikovsky's ballet, troikas in the snow, boats on the canals, carriages on the wide prospects, soirées and salons. A vanished time, captured and crystallized.

St Petersburg is a city that holds this magic for everyone. It excites feelings that in everyday life are left undisturbed. It is a mix of the strength of the Russian people, their remarkable sense of patriotism and the autocracy of the Tsars over such a huge expanse of land. Everywhere in the city each ruler has left his mark. The vaulting ambition of Peter the Great which founded this capital on a swamp; the realization of Empress Elizabeth's dreams of sumptuous luxury; Catherine's show of European good taste built in superior dimensions; Paul I's love of military order; his sons' admiration for classicism – right up to the more cosmopolitan styles at the end of the 19th century. And of course Lenin, Stalin, Kruschev and Brezhnev have followed suit and added their own stamp to this multi-faceted ancient capital.

It is important to have some idea of the melange of styles in St Petersburg in order to appreciate how the beautiful interiors, included in this book, are like oases. Step inside a perfectly restored palace of the century of your choice and you will find sanctuary from the chaos of Russian street life. Each one is a masterpiece, oozing memories of the past: jewels standing alone in the swamp.

The visitor to the city will discover they are not the only tourists. Most Russians think it important to take their children to St Petersburg so that they can appreciate the greatness of the Russian Empire with their own eyes. In Soviet days schoolchildren would be taken on compulsory excursions to see "the disgusting expense and flamboyance of the bourgeoisie" – such was the tone the tour guides would adopt – but they too appreciated the magnificence. From what I know from my contemporaries, these propaganda tours merely ignited their childhood imaginations. I experience this first hand every time my family name is mentioned; the thrill for Russians to meet a kniazhna (princess).

For obvious reasons I am most inspired by the Oranienbaum palaces, but every palace included in this book has tales of intrigue, romance and historical drama connected to them. In the following pages you will see a selection of palaces of different styles and periods, arranged in chronological order. Some

RIGHT: The first sight of Katalnaya Gorka (the Switchback Pavilion), appearing between the trees at Oranienbaum.

are famous, with hundreds of visitors passing through them every day. Others are only recently restored and open to the public at certain times of the year and a few are still secret treasures opened only for those in the know. The Grand Duke Vladimir's Palace for example, is well known to groups of present day Russian "intellectuals". I have been to private functions there, attempts at recreating the salons of former times: a talk on "the importance of psychiatry to modern art", a concert at which the local Marilyn Monroe lookalike sang and meetings of the "friends of Mayakovski" – a creative group made up of artists, musicians and local beauties. The style of entertainment may have changed with the times, but the location itself has not altered. In fact this palace has housed the Club for the Union of Scientists for the last 60 or so years and when you see the outstanding interior it is hard to believe that it is not a museum. It has the feel of a London gentleman's club, although Soviet scientists were not restricted by their sex. After a while, walking round freely, one can almost expect to meet with the party-loving Grand Duke himself.

The occasion that I felt most as though I had stepped into the past was seeing the Great Hall in the Catherine Palace filled with women in powdered wigs and 18th century gowns and with men in gold brocade and breeches. The mirrors all twinkled with the flicker of reflected lights and the parquet rang with the clip of buckled heeled shoes walking reverently up to present Christmas gifts to the Empress Elizabeth. A hushed silence fell on the court as the Tsarina spoke her thanks – only to be broken by the shouts of the camera crew as they moved in to get the next shot: this was an American production of the life of the young Catherine II. In order to raise money for the endless costs of restoration for these palaces the Tauride Palace, the Maryinsky Palace, Yelagin and even the palace of the Grand Duke Nicholas Nikolayevich have all recently been used for balls and banquets, as well as film sets. Natasha Rostov's first ball in the famous Bondarchuke version of 'War and Peace' was filmed in the Colonnade Hall of the Tauride Palace; the Rotunda in the Maryinsky Palace still holds performances for visiting heads of state and Yelagin is perfect for summer parties, with guests spilling into the surrounding park and music carrying over the Nevka river.

Once seen utilized in their proper manner these rooms lose their austerity and one can appreciate how they are built for such occasions. The dimensions are perfect, the floors are a pleasure to glide across and – a point so often forgotten in large spaces – the acoustics were always mathematically worked out so that music flows throughout the rooms as though through loud speakers and private conversations can be held despite the surrounding babble. The famous lengthy Russian speeches can reach the ends of even the longest galleries without the aid of a microphone. It is well worth privately testing your own voice in each room – you will be surprised at the effects: echoes, repetition, volume of which even the famous Feodor Chaliapin would be proud. Of course, even when these rooms are empty, one feels a sense of things past; the huddled groups of tourists seeming so incongruous amongst so much wealth.

During my time in Russia I have seen more changes than anyone can keep up with, and not only governmental. State money is no longer spent on keeping the Imperial palaces in their splendour. The people of St Petersburg are as proud as ever of their heritage, but it is hard to feel pride watching such treasures disintegrate by the month. Foreign investment has helped the lucky few, but in the present economic climate it is understandable that the city council prefers to save on gold leaf and spend on schools or public transport. It is a sorry state of affairs. Even Lenin, despite his eviction of the noble classes, encouraged the preservation of historical monuments – hence the enormous amount of restoration work after the Nazis bombed and destroyed much of the city and its environs during World War II. Many Soviet party bosses chose to keep the Romanov decor in their offices, thus preserving much of it, and no doubt such surroundings added to their own feelings of superiority.

The photographs and historical text of this book have secured some of the riches of this city forever, at a time when its future is uncertain. For those of you who have not yet seen the city of St Petersburg, this book will tempt you to venture into this magical land of contrasts and extinction. For those of you who have already experienced the wonders of its eclectic past, this volume is a reminder to you of some of the more unusual interiors. I hope everyone who opens these pages will feel that they have passed through doors into a unique and special world. A place that can conjure up all your dreams and fantasies. I am very glad that my family came from St Petersburg and so many of them helped to create such a heritage.

I would also like to thank Marie Clayton for involving me in this project. It is through her enthusiasm and love for the city of St Petersburg that this book has come into existence.

Princess Katya Galitzine
LONDON 1994

CHAPTER
ONE

The Catherine Palace

THE CATHERINE PALACE, a splendid building in the Imperial Baroque style, is in the town of Tsarskoye Selo 15 km outside St Petersburg. Tsarskoye Selo was renamed Pushkin in 1937, on the centenary of the poet's death. The original name is derived from the Swedish words, saari moisio, meaning a farmstead on a hill, which later became corrupted to Tsarskoye Selo which means 'village of the Tsar'. The palaces and parks here were designed over a period of 150 years by the leading architects of the day. This period saw many changes in both architectural and interior design style, and the Catherine Palace and park is a vast and unique complex, created by a wide variety of individual talents. Despite this, two architects in particular are closely associated with the Catherine Palace itself: Bartolommeo Rastrelli (1700-1771) and Charles Cameron (1743-1812).

Although it is often assumed that the Catherine Palace was named after Catherine the Great, she did not commission the building. In 1710 Peter the Great made a present of the area to his wife, the future Empress Catherine I. Some time later Catherine, in order to make the long absences of her husband more bearable, chose this spot to build a summer residence. This first building was a stone mansion with relatively simple decor, designed by Johann Friedrich Braunstein and Franz Ferster and built between 1718 and 1724. The design, a two storey block with sixteen rooms, was in itself a more up to date version of Jean-Baptiste Le Blond's central block at Peterhof. On Catherine's death this house passed to her daughter, the future Empress Elizabeth, who was at that time still an adolescent. She christened it the Catherine Palace after her beloved mother and, as the letter 'E' in Russian is the initial for both Ekaterina (Catherine) and Elizabeth, the monogram covered both names.

When Elizabeth finally came to the throne she was at last able to indulge her plans to enlarge the palace. Mikhail Zemtsov, together with his assistants Andrei Kvasov and Savva Chevakinsky, developed a broad programme for the reconstruction of the Tsarskoye Selo palace and park. Elizabeth insisted that the house built by her mother should be retained, so the major feature of the new palace was the addition of wings on either side of the original stone mansion, joined to the central building by single storey galleries. This had scarcely been completed in May 1752, when the Empress decided that the exterior was not sufficiently luxurious and the interiors unsuitable for large receptions and festivities. She proceeded to appoint Rastrelli to redesign the whole building.

Count Bartolommeo Francesco Rastrelli (the title was a papal one) was the son of an Italian sculptor, Count Carlo Bartolommeo Rastrelli, who had come to Russia with Le Blond in 1716. For twenty years Rastrelli not only designed all the larger government buildings, but also supervised all other architectural

activity in Russia and his genius is indelibly printed on Russian architecture of the mid 18th century. Rastrelli had a rare ability to combine elements from other styles into something not wholly derivative, nor entirely untraditional. It was fortunate that Rastrelli's imagination was matched by Elizabeth's taste, and the Catherine Palace became his masterpiece.

Elizabeth still insisted on preserving the central section, so Rastrelli had to find a way of adding larger state apartments to this modest core. He left the overall composition of the building designed by Zemtsov, but merged the different sections into a single building. He lengthened the façade to make it the longest in the world at that time: 298 metres. Unlike Peterhof, this tremendous range is unbroken by any significant projections or changes in height. To avoid the monotony of such a large surface, he liberally decorated it with columns, pilasters and statues.

For the long wings he adopted the powerful entrance motif of the Stroganov Palace: a series of alternate pairs of pilasters and boldly projecting engaged columns supporting broken pediments. The use of colour enlivens the endless expanse of columns and windows – the walls were originally painted grey-green (they are now bright blue), the architectural ornament white, and the figures of Atlas, the garlands, vases and the statues on the roof were gilded. Rastrelli used 100 kgs of pure gold for the exterior gilding, and contemporary visitors complained that their eyes were blinded by the palace on sunny days.

The most impressive view of the building is from the front courtyard: the immense extent of the façade, the play of light and shadow over the decoration, the rhythmical arrangement of snow white columns and pilasters against a background of rich colour, the intricate window surrounds, the bright detail of the sculptural elements and figures. Among the most impressive elements of the façade are the figures of Atlas, sixty large figures supporting the columns of the upper storey, and thirty-eight smaller ones supporting the arches over the French windows. The main entrance was originally placed at the far end of the building, so visitors had to drive past the entire length of the façade and had plenty of time to admire it. The courtyard was enclosed with semi-circular service wings and elaborate gates of gilded wrought iron by Giuseppe Corodoni, working to designs by Rastrelli.

The interior, in the style of the time, consists of a seemingly interminable succession of state rooms. The carved and gilded portals of the rooms, one after the other stretching into the distance, give the impression of a golden corridor. Rastrelli's contemporaries called this enfilade (which originally stretched the whole length of the palace before the main staircase was moved to the centre)

ABOVE: Detail of the rich carving and gilding of one of the lintel panels. Rastrelli used more than 100 kgs of pure gold in the interiors of the palace.

RIGHT: The carved and gilded portals of the rooms, one after the other stretching into the distance, give the impression of a golden corridor. Rastrelli's contemporaries called this enfilade 'The Golden Suite'.

PREVIOUS PAGE: The central section of the east façade of the Catherine Palace, which overlooks the gardens. This part of the Palace incorporates the original mansion built for Catherine I in 1718-24.

ABOVE: The Main Staircase, which was moved to its present position in the centre of the enfilade by Yuri Velten and Vasili Neyelov in 1779-92, was designed by Ippolito Monighetti in 1860-64.

'The Golden Suite': not only the doors but also the walls were decorated with intricate gilded carvings. More than 100 kgs of gold was used in the interior decoration.

The splendid effect of this passageway prepared the visitor for the breathtaking decor of the Great Hall. This room has a massive floor area of 846 sq m and the whole chamber is rich with the glow of gold. Daylight pours in through the double row of huge windows down each side of the hall and is reflected in the

mirrors set between each window. The frames are lavishly carved and gilded, caryatids and garlands of flowers, cherubs and baroque scrolls; the gold seems to flow round the room. All the decoration is hand carved in wood, Rastrelli would not use the cheaper and simpler stucco or plaster moulding. For official receptions and balls the hall was lit with 696 candles, set in sconces in front of the mirrors. The ceiling is painted with 'The Triumph of Russia', by Giuseppe Valeriani and Antonio Battista Peresinotti – the central section was repainted after World War II.

Rastrelli strove to use variety in the architectural and interior decoration of the palace. It was this search for the unusual and different which led to the decor of the Green Pilaster Room. The walls are divided up with pilasters, which are faced with green foil set behind clear glass. The gilding on the carved wood is of both bright and dull gold leaf, skillfully blended together. The skills required to do this, which were developed in Russia but lost over the ages, were revived by the restoration work. The ceiling features a painting of a military leader listening to Muses, by Stefano Torelli. The original perished during World War II and this is a replica created from drawings and photographs.

In the Crimson Pilaster Room the same decorative idea is repeated, but with red foil. The stove in this room is particularly unusual, it is faced with Russian tiles depicting fashions of the 18th century. Each tile has a different male or female dress style. The ceiling in this room is by an unknown 17th century Italian master, an original canvas evacuated before the war and entitled 'Alexander of Macedonia and the family of the Persian King, Darius'.

The Amber Chamber was once considered to be the "eighth wonder of the World". The amber wall panels were made for the royal palace at Charlottenburg and were presented to Peter the Great in 1717 by King Friedrich Wilhelm I. They were initially mounted in Peter the Great's small Winter Palace, then moved in the 1740s to the grand Winter Palace, before finally being installed in the Catherine Palace by Rastrelli. The original panels were too small for the room and too short for the high ceilings in the Catherine Palace, but Rastrelli found a simple solution. He set 24 narrow pilasters faced with mirror between the panels and installed a canvas frieze above them painted to match the amber, all decorated with richly gilded carving. The panels were made of small pieces of amber cunningly pieced together and decorated with mouldings in amber and altogether they weighed 800 kgs. When they were moved from St Petersburg to Tsarskoye Selo in 1755 they were so heavy, and so valuable, that Empress Elizabeth ordered that they were to be individually carried by veteran soldiers the entire distance. The panels were far too heavy to dismantle and

ABOVE: Detail of the lavishly gilded carving of one of the door frames in the Great Hall. All the decoration is hand carved in wood, Rastrelli would not use stucco moulding although it was cheaper and simpler.

RIGHT: Rastrelli's decorative fantasies reached their greatest fulfillment in the breathtaking decor of the Great Hall. Daylight pours in through the double row of huge windows each side and for official receptions it was also lit with 696 candles set in sconces in front of the mirrors.

evacuate before the Second World War. They went missing when the Catherine Palace was destroyed, but are believed to still exist and efforts are continually being made to track them down and restore them to their rightful place.

The decorative effect in the Picture Gallery was achieved by covering every inch of each of the side walls with paintings, separated only by narrow gilded frames. This hanging pattern was a common arrangement of the period, and the paintings are by well known European masters such as Jan Both, Antonio Balestra and Jacques Blanchard. The collection originally contained 130 pictures, mostly bought in 1745, of which 114 were evacuated and survived the war. When the room was restored the missing pictures were replaced by others of the same period and similar style. The beautiful floor in this room was restored to the original drawings by Rastrelli. The doors are considered to be the most splendid in the palace, caryatids support the lintel panels which depict Minerva and cupids surrounded with floral motifs.

Elizabeth's instinct was for excessive decoration, and the splendour of the Catherine Palace was marvelled at by the whole of Europe. The significance of Rastrelli's accomplishment for Russia lies in his creation of a consistent Russian version of the late Baroque, distinguished from its European counterparts by its scale, its exuberance and its use of colour.

When Elizabeth died in December 1761, Rastrelli's influence soon waned. The new Emperor, Peter III, was more interested in drilling troops than building palaces and his wife, the new Empress Catherine, had no more patience with Rastrelli's tastes than with those of Elizabeth. Rastrelli was suitably rewarded and departed in none too good a mood for Warsaw. Catherine's preference for a simpler style than Rococo was prompted as much by instinct as by her dislike of her aunt's taste. She was determined to alter matters drastically, and in a very short time she did.

Catherine used the framework created by Elizabeth and Rastrelli as State rooms to impress foreign visitors, but her own personal preference in her private life was for more comfortable and intimate apartments. Charles Cameron, a Scotsman, was the architect who eventually created the type of private rooms she had in mind. Cameron was the son of a London mason, and had been an apprentice carpenter and then an engraver. He was self-educated and became an accepted scholar of Roman civilization.

Cameron passed himself off as his aristocratic namesake, the famous Jacobean rebel Charles Cameron of Lochiel – this probably enabled him to catch the attention of Catherine II. He came to Russia in October 1779, and he succeeded in maintaining this deception until his death in 1812.

In 1780 the Empress issued an order: "all the construction work in the Imperial village (is) ... the responsibility of the architect Cameron brought from England." The man entrusted with this power had still not, at the age of 37, constructed any building. Cameron's first work at the Catherine Palace, after a few additions to the Chinese Village, was a series of private apartments. These rooms, known as the First, Fourth, and Fifth Apartments (confusingly there were no Second and Third), consisted essentially of the rearrangement and redecoration of suites within Rastrelli's old palace.

The Apartments, with the Agate Pavilion and the Cameron Gallery, were in the most strictly Classical interior style achieved in Russia up to that time. Cameron was a passionate admirer of Palladio and his designs were Roman and Pompeian in the manner known in Europe as 'Adam'. He used an extensive repertoire of Classical forms and motifs, and designed on an intimate, human scale which could also rise to a more austere antique dignity when the occasion

ABOVE: Detail of the carving on one of the pilasters. Restoration work after the Second World War revived ancient Russian skills which had been lost over the ages.

ABOVE: Each of the tiles on the stove in the Crimson Pilaster Room depicts a different male or female dress style of the 18th century.

RIGHT: Rastrelli's search for the unusual and different led to the decor of the Crimson Pilaster Room. The red of the pilasters is crimson foil set behind clear glass.

LEFT: The doors of the Picture Gallery are considered to be the most splendid in the palace. The lintel panels depict Minerva with cupids, surrounded with floral motifs.

RIGHT: The hanging pattern in the Picture Gallery was a common arrangement of the period. The collection originally contained 130 pictures of which 114 survived the Second World War.

demanded. Yet here was also a new and unexpected sumptuousness.

Cameron not only used the customary materials of NeoClassicism – moulded plaster reliefs, marble columns and wall facings, wood panelling and parquet floors – but went much further in his search for the precious and the exotic. He used semi-precious stones for wall panels, moulded glass for columns and ornaments, and flat panes of coloured or clear glass set on coloured felt to create shimmering surfaces. He also used bronze for the capitals and bases of his columns and a whole repertoire of decorative forms in ceramic and glass.

The First Apartment was an eight-room apartment created for the Grand Duke Paul and his wife Maria Feodorovna, in an area at the extreme north of the palace which had previously been occupied by a hanging garden designed by Rastrelli. The Green Dining Room is among the most Pompeian of Cameron's decorative schemes, the sumptuous stucco decoration was based on motifs from Pompeii frescoes of the 1st century AD. The chairs and the gilded bronze fire-dogs are original and were designed by Cameron specially for the room. Tables were only brought in when meals were about to be served. Drawings preserved in the Hermitage Museum show that Cameron submitted three sets of designs for this room to Catherine before she was satisfied.

The Bedchamber has a bed alcove outlined with groups of slim porcelain columns, with bases and capitals of gilt bronze. Further porcelain columns are set round the room beneath a frieze of stucco medallions on allegorical themes by Ivan Martos. The eight doors – some of which are purely decorative – are painted with arabesque designs.

The Choir Ante-room, which is next to the Church, has the most beautiful bright gold Lyon silk wallcovering, with delicate embroidery of pheasants, swans, peacocks and ducks. The embroidery was done by hand to the designs of Philippe de La Salle and took several years to complete. One of the Russian serfs who worked on the fabric has embroidered his name, Vasili Spider, discreetly in one corner. In the 19th century the original fabric had become worn, so it was put into storage and replaced with a copy. This replica was stolen during World War II, but the original survived the war in the store rooms of St Isaac's and has now been replaced.

The Study of Alexander I in this area was designed much later in 1818 by the Russian architect Vasili Stasov, in a simple and austere Classical style. The lower walls are of pale pink scagliola, the upper level is painted en grisaille with a frieze of Roman accoutrements and laurel leaves. Two Ionic columns are set on either side of the main entrance, two more flank the marble fireplace opposite. Lunettes depict Cupid and Psyche – family nicknames for Alexander I and his wife Elizabeth. The furnishings in this area have been completely restored after a watercolour by Alexei Korzukhin and from archive data.

The Fourth Apartment includes the Lyon Drawing Room, which took its name from the blue and white Lyon silk with which the walls were hung. Cameron used lapis lazuli from Lake Baikal for door frames and cornices in this area, while the floor was an intricate design in precious woods inlaid with mother of pearl. In the 1860s a set of lapis lazuli furniture was designed for the room by Monighetti. This room was destroyed during the Second World War and although some fragments of the floor have been recovered and some of the furniture was evacuated, it has not yet been restored.

The Fifth Apartment in the southern wing of the palace was Catherine's favourite and included her bedroom. This room was one of the most spectacular examples of Cameron's art, with richly three-dimensional decoration. The abundance of mirrors gave the effect of space and depth to the room. Tall columns of moulded glass were set on either side of the mirrors and the walls above were inset with Wedgwood plaques. Cameron lengthened the area by adding a hanging garden which Catherine could enter simply by opening her French windows, and which led to the Cameron Gallery and the Agate Pavilion.

ABOVE: Painted detail on one of the door panels of the Green Dining Room in the First Apartment (1780-3).

RIGHT: The sumptuous stucco decoration of the Green Dining Room is based on Pompeian motifs and was executed by Ivan Martos.

LEFT: The Bedchamber of the First Apartment is decorated with unusual slim porcelain columns. The bed alcove is outlined with groups of double columns supporting a half-canopy.

ABOVE: The stucco medallions on allegorical themes were made by Ivan Martos.

BELOW: Detail of the bottom of the porcelain columns, showing the gilt bronze bases and the delicate acanthus leaf decoration. The capitals of the columns are also of gilt bronze.

BELOW: Detail of one of the painted door panels. There are eight doors in the room, some of which are purely decorative.

RIGHT: The Study of Alexander I was designed in 1818 by the Russian architect Vasili Stasov in a simple and austere Classical style. The furnishings in this area have been completely restored after a watercolour by Alexei Korzukhin and from archive data.

ABOVE: Delicate embroidery of peacocks and ducks on the Lyon silk wallcovering of the Choir Ante-room next to the Church. The design also features pheasants and swans.

The apartment also included the Silver Study, and the Blue Snuff Box Room which had three beautiful pieces of lapis lazuli furniture. None of this area survived the war, although one of the lapis lazuli tables from the Blue Snuff Box Room was saved and is displayed in the Bedchamber of the First Apartment.

The Cameron Gallery is a glazed hall on the first floor of the Agate Pavilion, overlooking the park and with open colonnaded walkways on each side, in which Catherine could walk in rainy weather. Cameron wanted to create a feeling of Roman splendour in this area, and the walkways are lined with bronze

ABOVE: Lapis lazuli furniture by Monighetti, displayed on one of the floor panels from the Lyon Drawing Room in Fourth Apartment (1781-4). The floor had been taken to Berlin, where it was discovered rotting away under grain in a shed. There were only enough surviving fragments to reconstruct one panel.

busts of Greek philosophers and Roman emperors; to which Catherine added one of Charles James Fox because he was the opponent of William Pitt, Russia's adversary. The busts were copies of antique marble sculptures in the Hermitage.

Also on the first floor is the Great Hall, with the Agate Room and the Jasper Cabinet on either side. The Great Hall has plain white stucco walls, with eight contrasting fluted columns in grey-pink Olonets marble from Karelia which support the heavily ornate ceiling. Below the dado the walls are panelled in

RIGHT: Lapis lazuli decorative items, with the monogram of Maria Alexandrovna.

RIGHT: Lapis lazuli table by Monighetti, designed for the Lyon Drawing Room which has not yet been restored.

heavily veined dark grey-green marble. The large wall medallions, featuring mythological subjects, are by the sculptor Jacques Dominique Rachette. One fireplace was made in Italy with details in porphyry, the medallion above it is entitled 'Wedding'. The white Carrara marble fireplace with red Shoksha quartz was made in St Petersburg. The relief above this fireplace shows 'Alexander the Great breaking in Bucephalus'.

The Agate Room and the Jasper Cabinet are lavishly decorated with semi-precious stones from the Ural mountains. Only in Russia, with its wealth of natural stones, could Cameron have used these materials so generously. The walls and columns of the Agate Room are made of small pieces of red agate veined in white, cunningly pieced together. Its winding staircase leads down to the ground floor. The Jasper Cabinet has walls faced with panels of green jasper, with green jasper mouldings, while its columns are of red agate. The variety of different hues and tones in the natural stone creates a wonderfully rich effect, which is made even more opulent with painting, ornate mouldings and gilded bronze. The furniture was all Pompeian in style, very imposing but rather hard and formal. The floors are inlaid with palissander (a type of rosewood) and palm wood. These rooms survived the occupation because the first floor was used as the German officers' club, but they have not been fully restored and are generally sealed for conservation reasons.

On the ground floor beneath was an elaborate suite of baths, based on the Roman models of Titus and Diocletian. The Frigidarium had a large tin swimming pool, while next to it were comfortable rooms with divans, open fires and warm baths. One of these baths was in white marble, copied from a Roman model, and had a stone canopy supported by four columns and taps of gilded bronze. The area was decorated with beautiful moulding by Rachette. The ground floor was destroyed when it was used as stables by the German army and again has not yet been restored.

When Catherine was older she suffered from gout and rheumatism and it became painful for her to go up and down the staircase at the end of the Cameron Gallery. The Scotsman then built her a pente douce – a gentle sloping ramp which allowed her to reach the garden from her first floor apartment without effort. The words entered the Russian language: 'pandus' means a slope of this sort.

Cameron also brought to Russia a sense of colour which became an inherent part of the new Classicism. The brilliant blues and golds, the strong clear hues which had characterized the Catherine Palace at the time of Elizabeth, went out of fashion. Primary colours were replaced by complementary ones or by muted

TOP: The columns of grey-pink Karelia marble in the Main Hall of the Agate Pavilion (1780-5) were done by Alexei Kochetov.

ABOVE: The elaborate floor design is inlaid in a variety of precious woods.

OPPOSITE: The ceiling is both vaulted and divided into an elaborate geometric design of different shaped panels with gilded gesso framing. Each panel is either painted or moulded - mainly with dancing female figures.

ABOVE: Ceiling of the Jasper Cabinet, with its elaborate Pompeian decoration. The rooms of the Agate Pavilion have not been restored and are generally closed for conservation reasons.

tones, bronze for gold, lavender for blue, olive and pistachio for bright green, and grey-blue for Elizabeth's favourite azure.

Cameron was well known for his refusal to stand on ceremony. Grand Duchess Maria Feodorovna, for whom Cameron worked at Pavlovsk, wrote to her agent: "You know very well from experience that mildness gets you nowhere with Cameron, but please tell him that he is unbearable and that he should take care." Upsetting the Grand Duchess and her husband did Cameron no good: after Catherine's death he was summarily dismissed by Paul I. He stayed in Russia, however, and came back into favour when Alexander I came to the throne.

In 1820 the Russian ambassador, Prince Lieven, acquired 114 of Cameron's drawings to be used by Stasov in restoring the apartments at the Catherine Palace which had been damaged by fire. They were to prove invaluable during the loving restoration of Cameron's buildings after the terrible damage done during the Second World War.

CHAPTER
TWO

THE CHINESE PALACE

In an area about 29 km west of St Petersburg, on the southern shores of the Gulf of Finland, is the palace of Oranienbaum. The Main Palace was built by Peter the Great's favourite courtier, Alexander Menshikov, after Peter had established a Summer palace for himself at nearby Peterhof. The name Oranienbaum means 'orange tree', which in cold and wintry Russia symbolized everything that was scarce, extremely luxurious and available only to the aristocracy. The palace built by Menshikov was not only bigger and more impressive than the Tsar's, it was also decorated much more luxuriously. After the death of Peter the Great and his wife, Catherine I, Menshikov fell into disgrace and was sent into exile, where he died in 1729 having had all his property confiscated.

When Empress Elizabeth I came to the throne, she gave Oranienbaum to her nephew and successor Peter and his young wife Catherine as their summer palace. Chosen by Elizabeth as a suitable bride for Peter, Catherine had taken to her adopted country. She changed her name from Sophia to Catherine (after Elizabeth's mother) and converted to Russian Orthodoxy. She worked hard to learn the language and be accepted by the Russians: "I tried as much as I could to win the hearts of the people with whom I was to spend my life."

Much later, after Catherine had deposed her husband Peter III and was ruler of the Russian Empire and mistress of Oranienbaum, she decided to build a small private summer house. Far behind the Main Palace, on a plateau, lay an upper park where things had been left to grow wild. Catherine found this area charming, and she commissioned Rinaldi to build the Chinese Palace there.

Antonio Rinaldi (c1709-1794), who had studied with the famous Italian architect Luigi Vanvitelli, had been brought to Russia by Cyril Razumovsky, the younger brother of Elizabeth's morganatic husband, Alexei Razumovsky. Rinaldi was one of Peter III's favourite architects, so by rights Catherine should have disliked him, but luckily she recognized his talent. The first work that he did at Oranienbaum – a hall for theatrical performances and a Chinese Pavilion – have not survived, but the Chinese Palace is one of the most complete examples of his work in existence in Russia.

The Palace was originally called the Dutch House or Little House in the Upper Park, but by the end of the 18th century it was generally known as the Chinese Palace – although at first appearance it seems to be remarkably unoriental. The exterior in sombre and elegant Italianate style is distinctly European, and there is nothing Chinese about the Great Hall. In fact the name comes from the unusual and exotic Chinese decoration used in the rooms in the west wing.

The Palace was designed as a low one-storey building, with side pavilions connected by short wings. The second storey with a glass roofed gallery was added later in 1852-53 by Andrei Stakenschneider. An enfilade of reception rooms runs along the main north front. In the centre is the Great Hall, which breaks forward in a canted bay from the façade. This is flanked on each side by two smaller rooms leading to another great reception room, at one end the Hall of Muses and at the other the Large Chinese Room. Two wings run back from the enfilade, each containing a suite of bedroom, sitting room, cabinet and closet, and in between them is the small entrance vestibule.

Inside it is not particularly splendid or richly decorated, but everything is delicate and exquisite. For the decor Rinaldi surrounded himself with true artists, including Stefano Torelli – who had been in Russia for 22 years – and the Barozzi brothers, Giuseppe and Serafino, from Bologna. They trained Russian pupils and founded a school of artisans that produced the most wonderful stucco work.

As one passed through the vestibule, the Great Hall was meant to dazzle the visitor with its unexpected size, its colour and the richness of its decoration. The ceiling has delicate plasterwork in pink, grey, white and gilt and originally in the centre there was a mythological painting called the 'Triumph of Mars' by Giambattista Tiepolo, who was commissioned by the Russian Court. This painting was removed for safekeeping before World War II and then vanished. A canvas of similar size and shape, 'Day Driving Away Night' by Torelli, was later taken from the Marble Palace to replace it. The walls are covered with a range of blue and pink scagliola, set off by gilt ornaments and punctuated with paintings of 'Diana and Endymion' and 'The Rape of Ganymede' and 'Juno' by Torelli.

It is unlikely the subject matter was left to chance, especially as the twin bas-reliefs of Peter the Great and Elizabeth over the main doors, by Marie-Anne Collot, suggest that the room was imbued with a certain symbolism. Catherine constantly identified herself with these two great former rulers of Russia, possibly to forestall any question of her claim to the throne. One could interpret Juno, Empress of the Gods, as Catherine, Empress of Russia. The other two paintings both tell the story of a lowly youth who was loved by a goddess – as Catherine at the time loved Grigory Orlov, an officer of the Guards who came from humble stock.

It would not have been suitable to place such symbolism in a public place, but the Chinese Palace was Catherine's private retreat; she called it her dacha, and it was sometimes referred to as as 'The Empress's Solitude'. When the palace

LEFT: The oval relief of Peter the Great over the doors in the Great Hall is by Marie-Anne Collot. Collot was a pupil of Étienne-Maurice Falconet and also his daughter-in-law. The background to the relief is in blue and red smalt glass, decorated with gilded copper and enamel.

PREVIOUS PAGE: The Chinese Palace is set in a wooded area in the upper park at Oranienbaum.

LEFT: The trellis motif used in the ceiling and floor decoration of the Pink Parlour is one of the earliest examples of its kind in Russia.

ABOVE: Detail of the beautiful floor design of the Damask Bedroom.

was built, such retreats would inevitably have been in the company of her lover. Perhaps this identification of the Chinese Palace with Orlov, with whom she broke in 1772, explains why she seldom used the Palace in the latter part of her reign. In all she probably visited it about 50 times in 30 years.

The Great Hall has suffered badly from damp, which has been a problem at the Chinese Palace for 100 years. The building was originally protected by a

ABOVE: The Damask Bedroom, which was designed for Catherine's son the Grand Duke Paul, is draped in pale green silk which is an exact reproduction of the original fabric.

RIGHT: The ceiling of the Boudoir features 'Psyche and Flora' by Jacopo Guarana, who also did the three wall paintings entitled 'Music', 'Painting' and 'Drama'.

ABOVE: Detail of the delicate garlands of flowers painted on the wall panelling by Serafino Barozzi.

LEFT: The tiny Boudoir at the end of the east wing is entirely panelled in polished walnut and the whole room is darkly rich and opulent.

complex drainage system and has no damp course, but this system has deteriorated over the years causing damp to rise into the building. In the 19th century the Great Hall was painted white, probably to disguise the effects of damp. It was restored in the 1960s, but all round the walls can be seen a subtle tidemark where the new work does not quite match the old. It is hoped in due course to do this work again, but it is not easy to match scagliola.

The Pink Parlour to the east of the vestibule has unusual painted fabric walls. These have been plain pink since the 19th century, but originally were on canvas and included pictures by Serafino Barozzi. The floor and ceiling decoration uses a trellis motif; this is one of the earliest examples of this motif in Russia. The furniture is all original, the carved and gilded items were made in Russia, while the marquetry work comes from Holland, England and France.

The suite of rooms in the east wing was meant for Catherine's young son, Grand Duke Paul. The Damask Bedroom is draped in pale green silk fabric, which is an exact reproduction of the original fabric done after the Second

World War. The fabric was produced by hand, and it took three Russian women 10 years to complete. The floor design is particularly beautiful, with a trellis motif decorated with flowers. The ceiling was originally in scagliola, which was painted over in the 19th century, and has a central painting of 'Urania teaching a Youth' by Domenico Maggiotto.

The tiny Boudoir at the end of the east wing is entirely panelled in polished walnut, painted with delicate garlands of flowers by Serafino Barozzi. The doors are decorated with the figures of Diana and Mars. The floor is again a very intricate design in inlaid wood and the whole room is darkly rich and opulent. The beautiful marquetry furniture was made in Holland and France.

The Hall of Muses or Picture Gallery is light and airy, with its rows of French windows down each side leading out into the garden. It is a frothy confection of pinks and blues, of flowing plasterwork and allegorical figures of the Muses. It looks as if it has been transported straight from Italy, not surprisingly it was indeed painted by an Italian: Stefano Torelli. The ceiling is painted with sensual scenes, featuring Venus and the Graces with various male figures.

All the rooms in the Chinese Palace astonish the visitor with their exquisite detail, but none more so than the Bugle Bead Room which leads from the east wing to the Great Hall. This is decorated with embroidery hangings designed by Frenchman Jean Pillement, beautiful and detailed work showing exotic birds set against a fantasy landscape. The background to the design is made up entirely of tiny silvered glass bugle beads and the light shimmers and flows over the walls. Each hanging is set in a gilded frame heavily carved in the shape of a garlanded palm tree, while above each hanging is a small carved dragon. In the room are tables of brightly coloured smalt glass mosaic, made in the Ust-Ruditsk works near St Petersburg by Mikhail Lomonosov (who had revived the lost art of glass mosaic work). These tables were specially made for the room and were originally complemented by a floor made of the same material, thus the room was originally called the Mosaic Room in the 18th century. The floor took five years to complete and it is hard to imagine a more gorgeous but less practical floor surface; it is not surprising that it was so badly damaged by the 1850s that it had to be replaced with the present inlaid wood floor. The interior of this room must be one of the most magical ever created and during the long days of the Russian summer the daylight pouring through the windows bounces from wall to wall and back again.

RIGHT: The light and airy Hall of Muses, with decor by Stefano Torelli, looks as if it was transported straight from Italy.

ABOVE: Detail of the wall hangings. The bugle beads were hand sewn onto the hangings by nine Russian girls from nearby St Petersburg under the supervision of the Frenchwoman Madame de Chéne. The exotic designs of birds and fantasy scenes are embroidered in chenille thread on canvas.

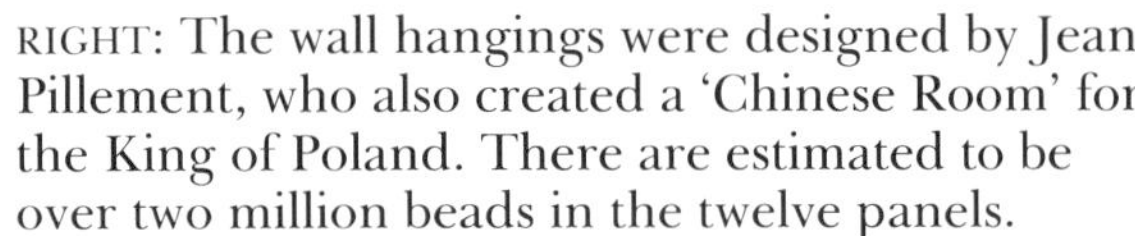

RIGHT: The wall hangings were designed by Jean Pillement, who also created a 'Chinese Room' for the King of Poland. There are estimated to be over two million beads in the twelve panels.

The exotic birds and buildings on the hangings in the Bugle Bead Room give the first indication of the East, but the rooms on the other side of the Great Hall in the western end of the enfilade provide the full reason for the Chinese name.

The Small Chinese Room is remarkable above all for its colour scheme, quite unlike contemporary European colours. The reds, greens and dark blues, highlighted with gold, that predominate give it a very rich and opulent feeling. Chi-

ABOVE: The Small Chinese Room is remarkable for its colour scheme, quite unlike contemporary European colours. Chinese motifs are used for all the decorative framing and panelling, while the walls are covered with Chinese silk.

nese motifs are used for all the decorative framing and panelling, while the walls are covered with Chinese silk. The floor is one of the most attractive on the palace, with its design of Chinese latticework and bowls of flowers. Rinaldi was not fond of geometric designs and he very rarely used them, but they are employed to great effect here.

The Small Chinese Room is only a taster for the breathtaking Large Chinese

ABOVE: Detail of one of the fantasy oriental scenes on the walls of the Large Chinese Room. The designs are all beautifully inlaid in wood.

Room beyond. This was entirely created by the Barozzi brothers and has no equal in Europe. The walls are of inlaid wood, designed as fantasy oriental landscape scenes. The intricate design of the marquetry floor sweeps and turns in a riot of movement. In the ceiling the 'Marriage of Europe and Asia' by Barozzi perhaps symbolizes the great land mass of Russia, stretching from central Europe far into Asia. Chinese furniture, made to Western models, lines the walls and large pieces of Chinese porcelain are placed on cabinets and chimneypiece. The great wooden billiard table, stamped with the English name 'Clarke', is in a rather Gothic style and it seems somewhat out of place in such an exotic setting. In fact it pre-dates the Chinese Palace and comes from the earlier Menshikov Palace.

The rooms in the west wing were designed for Catherine herself. At the moment the astonishing Chinese Bedroom with its array of mirrors is hidden from view, due to the restoration work being carried out. Only the ceiling, a painting of 'The Chinese Offering' by Jacopo Guarana can be seen.

The Boudoir in the west wing has 11 pastel portraits of the Ladies in Waiting of the Court, painted by the Frenchman Jean de Sampsoy. These were designed to represent the seasons, the elements and other symbols of nature. There are geographical symbols used in the floor design, and the ceiling features a painting entitled 'Geography' by Gasparo Diziani. The Portrait Room beyond is decorated with 23 fashionable paintings of heads by Pietro Rotari. The ceiling has a painting of 'Innocence and Wisdom' by Giovanni Battista Pittoni.

The tiny Gold Study at the end of the west wing served as a small library for Catherine. The ceiling painting of 'History' by Diziani is certainly meant to indicate that serious work would be done in this room. The beautiful wall murals depicting 'Selene and Endymion', 'Venus and Paris' and 'Mercury', by Stefano Torelli, had been painted over at some period and were only uncovered in 1964. The Gold Study takes its name from the gilded background to the walls and the gilded ornamentation to the panels by Barozzi.

Most of the supervising craftsmen at the Chinese Palace were Italian, but most of the workmen were Russian and the majority of the furniture was made

RIGHT: The breathtaking Large Chinese Room was created by the Barozzi brothers and has no equal in Europe.

LEFT: The tiny Gold Study was meant as a library for Catherine. The beautiful wall murals had been painted over at some period and were only uncovered in 1964.

RIGHT: The extravagant and beautiful Switchback Pavilion (Katalnaya Gorka), set in the park at Oranienbaum, looks rather like a heavily iced wedding cake.

in workshops in St Petersburg. The Chinese Palace proved that the Russian Court was aware of the latest trends in European architecture. The Chinese style, so thoroughly unoriental and which by a curious inverted process reached Russia not directly from the East but the long way round from China through Europe, enjoyed an international vogue in the 1750s and 1760s. Although its exotic details are less conspicuous, the Oranienbaum pavilion is not so far removed in spirit or date from Frederick the Great's tea-house at Potsdam.

THE SWITCHBACK PAVILION, also situated in the park at Oranienbaum, is one of the most original of all the pavilions. It was designed by Rinaldi, and originally incorporated a long 'rollercoaster' to one side. From the Pavilion participants used to embark on a precipitous descent down the artificial slope – which was known as a 'montagne russe' – on a specially designed little cart on rails. Artificial hills like these were popular attractions at fairs and public parks and were also often built in ice and snow in winter for tobogganing; in a country as flat as the area around St Petersburg, even such a slight elevation provoked a sensation of height and speed.

The 'montagne russe' at Oranienbaum was a more permanent structure, built for use only during the summer months. It incorporated a raised promenade down both sides so that those not taking part could admire the action – and of course cheer wildly when the Empress took a turn. A visiting Englishman, Archdeacon Coxe, described it in 1784 as 'the mountain of sledges'. The actual rollercoaster has long since disappeared, demolished in the 19th century when it became unsafe, but Rinaldi's two-storey pavilion remains as an wonderful example of late 18th century pleasure architecture.

This extravagant but beautiful folly, with its pyramid shape and heavily decorated with columns, balustrades, and decorative urns, looks rather like an iced wedding cake. Rinaldi designed the building in a simple Classical style, but added Baroque details – there are over 100 decorative urns and originally there were also gilded statues. The walls of the first floor are decorated with rather severe pilasters, while the surrounding verandah on the floor below has alternate paired and single Doric columns. Only the crowning element – a slender tapering dome somewhat like a Chinese hat – is at all exotic.

ABOVE: Detail of the painted decoration on the door panels.

Inside the pavilion guests relaxed or watched from the balconies as others played. The plan recalled the Baroque layouts of an earlier age, with a central circular hall and three square wings. The Rotunda on the first floor is a wonderfully light and airy room, with a beautiful scagliola floor in delicate pinks, blues and greens by Spinelli after drawings by Rinaldi. The ceiling is a trompe l'oeil design of flowers and grapes on a trellis by Serafino Barozzi. The walls are painted tempera on plaster, decorated with garlands of flowers and leaves. The door panels are also painted, while the three paintings over the doors – depicting 'Neptune', 'Amphitrite', and 'Nereid on a Dolphin' – were painted by Stefano Torelli.

The Porcelain Study in one wing displays 28 porcelain groups, specially modelled for this room by Meissen, which are mainly allegories of the Russian Navy's victory over Turkey at Chesme in 1770. The figures are unique, as the moulds were destroyed after the series was made. The plaster scrollwork of the wall panels is designed to sweep into a series of shelves, some shaped as cherub's heads, monkeys or eaglets. Each porcelain group sits on its own special shelf and the entire decoration of the room was designed to complement the

LEFT: The Rotunda on the first floor is a wonderfully light and airy room, decorated in delicate pinks, blues and greens by Spinelli, Serafino Barozzi and Stefano Torelli.

RIGHT: Detail of the beautiful scagliola floor of the Rotunda by Spinelli, after drawings by Rinaldi. This is now in need of some restoration work.

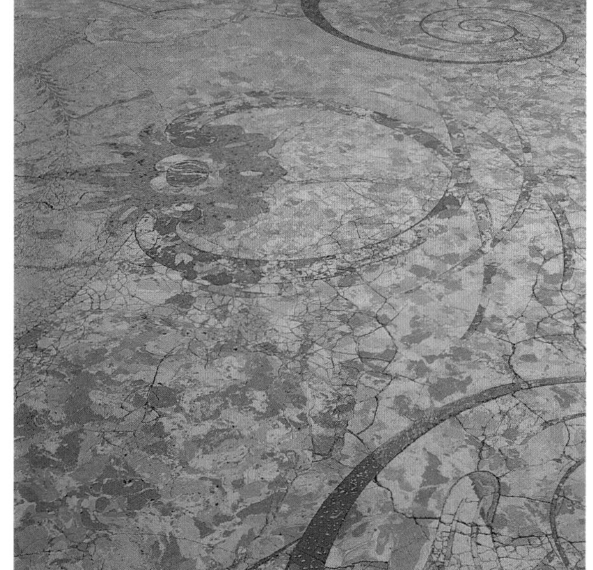

LEFT: The ceiling of the Porcelain Study is a trompe l'oeil design with cherubs.

RIGHT: The Porcelain Study displays 28 Meissen groups, which were made specially for this room. They mainly depict allegories of the Russian Navy's victory over Turkey at Chesme in 1770.

colours of the china. The floor has a border frieze of parquet, designed to focus attention on the central painted area. The frieze is original, but the central area has been repainted.

The White Study is subtly decorated with a variety of shades of white moulding against a pale turquoise background. The scagliola floor is in the same delicate colours. The original moulding of the 18th century has survived surprisingly well in this room.

The third wing contains the staircase from the ground floor, and originally also led out to the verandah and the 'montagne russe'. The area on the ground floor is now used as a display room and includes a beautifully detailed model of the Switchback Pavilion, complete with 'montagne russe'.

Although the Chinese Palace and the Switchback Pavilion have been open to Russians since 1922, even today very few Europeans have visited them. The Chinese Palace is not only one of the most sumptuous of all 18th century European buildings, it is also unique among St Petersburg's suburban palaces because it is almost entirely original. The whole area suffered terribly during the siege of Leningrad in the Second World War. The Germans blockaded the

ABOVE: The beautifully detailed model of the Switchback Pavilion, complete with 'montagne russe', was made after the original drawings for the building by Rinaldi.

city for three years, and in this period over a million inhabitants lost their lives. When the fighting ceased and the Germans withdrew, the surrounding area had been devastated by the shelling and the great Imperial palaces were left in ruins. But Oranienbaum remained a Russian enclave and was never captured, so both the Chinese Palace and the Switchback Pavilion survived unharmed while their contents – which had been evacuated – remained intact. Of course there was some damage from decay and neglect during the war period, but most of this has now been fully repaired and restored. The lasting impression of both buildings is not of skillful restoration, but of the remarkable survival of two beautiful and complete examples of Rinaldi's work.

CHAPTER THREE

GATCHINA PALACE

GATCHINA, A TOWN OF IMPERIAL PALACES, pavilions and follies, lies 45 km south-west of St Petersburg. Originally built as the country residence of that noble sybarite Grigory Orlov, it became a fortified military town during the "exercise in patience" as Crown Prince Paul waited for his mother Catherine II to die. The combination of the skills of Rinaldi and Brenna made Gatchina into one of the finest examples of early Russian NeoClassicism. Its design and layout were basically set within the 35 years from 1766 to 1801, and in the rest of its two-hundred year history only slight modifications were made to the original design: traditionally the Russian emperors tried to maintain the designs of their predecessors intact if possible.

The area once belonged to the great principality of Novgorod and was first mentioned in the chronicle of 1499 as Khotchino village on the Khotchino lake. In the course of the Swedish-Livonian war the lands were conquered by the Swedes, but by 1721 – during the reign of Peter the Great – they were recovered.

A small Swedish farmstead there was granted by Tsar Peter to his younger sister Natalia, upon whose death the estate passed to another owner. By 1732 it was registered as part of the Crown lands and in 1734 Empress Anna Ioannovna, Peter's niece, presented the estate to Chancellor Prince Boris Kurakin. When Kurakin died in 1765 his relations announced the sale of the country house, along with 20 villages, to pay his debts. Catherine II acted promptly and bought Gatchina to present it straight to her lover Grigory Orlov. The latter was absolutely thrilled with the gift and decided to build himself a castle in the wilderness, as he wanted to get away from the festivities at Tsarskoye Selo and escape the intrigues of the Imperial court to spend time in the company of close friends and keen hunters.

Count Orlov selected Antonio Rinaldi (c1709-1794) as the architect for his castle and its interior. Rinaldi stood high in the favour of the Empress Catherine and he had gained experience of castle architecture during the planning and initial construction of a huge castle at Cascerta, near Naples, built to the plans of his teacher Luigi Vanvitelli. He also knew English castle architecture which he had studied during his travels in England.

On May 30 1766 the foundation stone was laid; in all the construction works lasted for 15 years. The palace is set at the highest point of the surrounding landscape. The central main building has curved galleries sweeping forward from either side, each ending in a square wing with a tower at the corner: the Kitchen wing was to the east and the Arsenal to the west. The Kitchen wing was occupied by the household staff, while the Arsenal was originally the stables.

The Classical north façade is 270m long and curves round the parade

RIGHT: Gatchina is a very romantic castle, with numerous towers and a secret passage, set in beautiful countryside.

ground in front of the palace. The walls are faced with an inexpensive local limestone of greyish-yellow colour; the naturally soft limestone was easy to cut and finish, but became incredibly hard and durable after exposure to the elements. Rinaldi's decision to use this local material, rather than following the established tradition of finishing the walls in stucco painted different colours, probably indicates that he sought the opinion of local professionals.

The façade has clear horizontal divisions – the ground floor is decorated with Doric pilasters, the first floor with double Ionic pilasters, the second floor is lined with plain panels separated by simple grooved bands. Window and arch surrounds are only set slightly forward from the main wall face and are barely visible. The palace front has 79 windows on each floor, 29 of them in the main building; the dark passageways typical of old castles do not exist here. The north façade central portico is decorated with a plaque: "Founded on May 30, 1766, finished in 1781".

The south façade overlooking the garden is reminiscent of Richmond Palace and of castles in the south of England – or such was the impression of Stanislaus Poniatovsky, the last king of Poland, who visited Gatchina in 1797. The ex-king also mentioned numerous towers in the style of English castles. Gatchina also has a romantic secret: an underground passageway, which led towards the Silver Pond to end up in Echo Grotto and was constructed as an amusement. In 1917 the passage was used by Alexander Kerensky, the ex-chairman of the Provisional government, to escape when mutinous soldiers took Gatchina by storm.

During the construction Catherine II often arrived to stay for days with her "Gatchina landlord", as she nicknamed Grigory. According to the Kammerfouriere – the register of every minute in the day of the Empress – endless meals were served and they passed their time boating, strolling along pathways, playing cards alfresco, falcon hunting, and shooting game. The telescopes which Orlov collected were set on the flat roofs of the castle observation towers and offered spectacular views of the rolling grounds and fine old forests. In 1777 the Empress paid her last visit to look at the almost completed building – by this time Potyomkin had already replaced Orlov as her favourite.

After Orlov's death in 1783 the whole of the Gatchina residence, with its outbuildings and furnishings, was purchased by Catherine from Orlov's family for 1,500,000 rubles. The ukaze – or order of the monarch – dated August 6 1783 announced that Gatchina was granted to the Crown Prince Paul on the occasion of his daughter Alexandra's birth. Paul accepted the gift with gratitude, although he normally hated everybody whom his mother liked and despised the places associated with her lovers. Orlov was an exception; Grigory had always treated little Paul with sympathy and had given him lessons on how to operate a telescope. Barred from politics, Paul had taken up military matters, and Gatchina was also ideal as the headquarters of his small private army of Prussian style soldiers.

Vincenzo Brenna (1747-1819), a Classicist and a favourite court architect of Paul, considerably altered Rinaldi's building. Brenna was born in Florence and had been educated in Rome and Paris. He was introduced to the heir to the Russian throne in Poland in 1782, where he had completed several brilliant decorative paintings in various castles. By 1784 Brenna was Charles Cameron's assistant at Pavlovsk, which was being built for Paul and his wife Maria Feodorovna. Paul liked Brenna's manner and his preference for the Roman Imperial style.

At Gatchina Brenna used the existing framework created by Rinaldi, but enlarged upon it and imposed his own style. He increased the height of the towers, the main block and the curving galleries, he also changed many of the interiors. The first floor rooms of the main building were for the Emperor, the Empress and for State receptions, while the ground floor accommodated Paul's private apartments. The rooms are of an overall Classical design, with decorative references to Ancient Rome, the Italian Renaissance, and 17th century France.

ABOVE: Off the Antechamber a small lobby displays a marble relief of Antonio Rinaldi with a pair of compasses in hand, by the sculptor Fedot Shubin.

On the first floor the Antechamber, a square room of 55 sq m, was originally designed by Rinaldi. Here courtiers waited for Tsar Paul to appear each morning and also the daily changing of the guard took place. Although Brenna considerably changed the design at the end of the 18th century, Rinaldi's imprint still manifests itself in the general composition, the deeply coved ceiling, the cornice design with dentils, the wide door architraves of smooth rose Breccia scagliola, the polished and inlaid doors. The room features one of Rinaldi's best inlaid floor patterns: a central diamond surrounded with curving bands, semi-spirals, exotic flower shapes and acanthus fronds.

The ceiling originally contained an allegorical painting depicting Bellona, the goddess of war, surrounded with Glory and Power and with invincible Mars kneeling before her. The subject matter was undoubtedly meant to symbolize either Catherine or Russia. Unfortunately this painting perished in the fire in 1944 and it has been replaced with the decorative 'Love and Faithfulness' by an unknown 18th century master, which was brought from the store rooms of the Russian Museum.

The walls are divided into rectangular panels by bands of ornamental moulding with a relief of a helmet set in each corner. The lintel panels have a stylized floral design with nymphs and a lyre. In the 19th century three paintings were displayed here: 'Expulsion from Paradise' by Luca Giordano, 'Tempest' by Joseph Vernet and a portrait of Emperor Paul dressed as the Grand Master of the Knights of Malta by Salvatore Toncci. All these pictures were evacuated before the Second World War and have survived, although they have not yet been returned to their rightful places.

The ceiling and coving are decorated with mouldings of garlands, antique helmets, shields, banners and Roman eagles – military symbols designed to complement the ceremonial uniforms and epaulettes paraded daily through the room.

The central White Hall is the largest of all the restored rooms, 120 sq m in area. It is a light and airy room, with its row of five French windows which lead out onto a terrace overlooking the front parade ground. The ceiling once had a central painting of 'Hercules at the cross-roads, between Vice and Virtue', painted by Giuseppe Bonito, an 18th century master from Naples. It was installed into a massive stucco frame against a trellis background with cruciferae flowers. The picture was a gift from Catherine II to her son – perhaps intended as a morally improving gesture! It disappeared during the German occupation and has been replaced with an original painting, 'Birth of a Hero' by Frenchman Gabriel Doyen which was painted in 1798 on the birth of the Grand Duke Michael Pavlovich. This new painting was taken from the store rooms of the Hermitage. The trellis motif, the masks, and the shells at the corners of the ceiling are typical of Brenna.

The White Hall is famous, however, for its moulded stucco ornamentation after Rinaldi's drawings. Moulded stucco was one of Rinaldi's favourite decorative devices, and he brought the art to perfection. The ceiling coving features an elaborate composition of a stylized shell against a pair of crossed and flaming torches, with flowing fronds of acanthus leaves, flower garlands festooned with ribbons, and rosettes. In each corner is a shell with a mask of the goddess Flora wearing a laurel wreath.

The architect Grim, a late 19th century art historian, believed that the unknown stucco craftsmen working under Rinaldi were genuine and gifted artists in their own right. Although Rinaldi probably supplied a draft outline of the general composition of ornaments and dimensions, within this framework the craftsman was free to add detailed flowers and buds, to lavishly curve fronds and twist ribbons. The lily is a common motif in the decoration of the White Hall: long stems of lily are crossed on wall panels and are woven into wreaths, a lily can be seen on the lintel panel and in the garlands on the coving.

RIGHT: The Antechamber was originally designed by Rinaldi, although Brenna altered it considerably at the end of the 18th century. The room features one of Rinaldi's best inlaid floor designs.

RIGHT: Contemporary painting of the changing of the guard in the Antechamber.

RIGHT: The design of this lintel panel, with the lobsters creeping out of rocks and weeds and surrounded with delicious fruit and exotic flowers, owes more to the imagination of the craftsman than to the real life. The other lintel panel in the White Hall shows a lion with shrubs and a corn sheaf.

FAR RIGHT: Detail of one of the beautifully inlaid door panels.

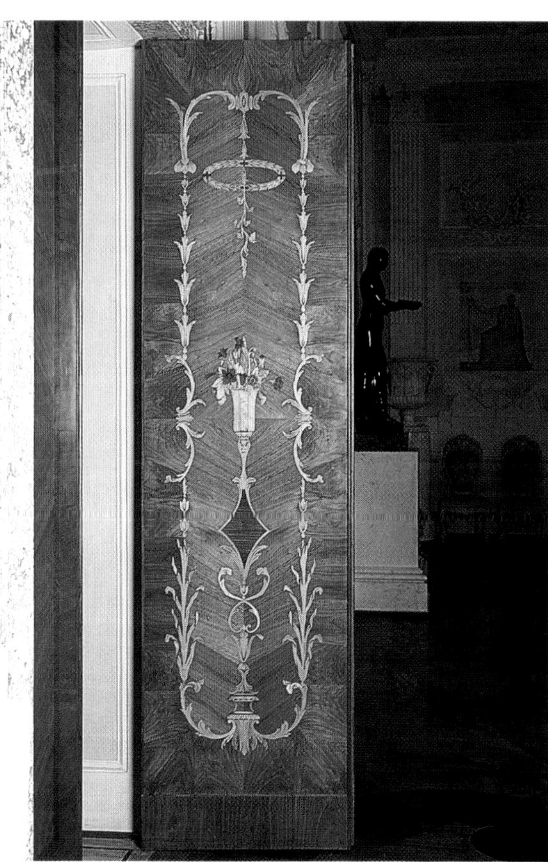

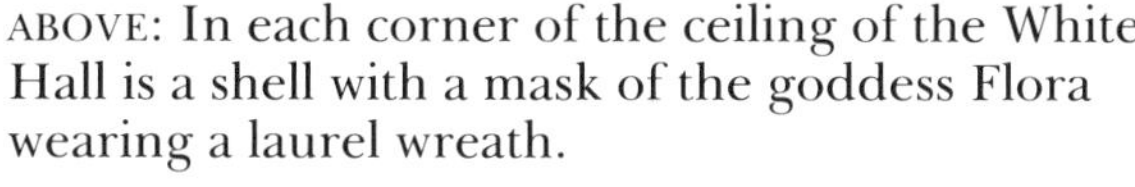

ABOVE: In each corner of the ceiling of the White Hall is a shell with a mask of the goddess Flora wearing a laurel wreath.

LEFT: The White Hall is the largest of the restored rooms and is famous for its moulded stucco designs which were executed by craftsmen straight onto wall or coving. The windows are set back in bays decorated with rosettes.

The lily is recognized as Rinaldi's flower, although in fact it was probably the favourite flower of the particular craftsman who applied the stucco moulding on site.

The floor design, which has been restored after drawings by Rinaldi, would originally have echoed the ceiling design but it has little in common with Brenna's redesigned ceiling. Only the general composition and a few details are similar: an oval, a half-oval, trellis work, and curved acanthus fronds. The major part of the background design is in mahogany, with stylized rings and semi-ovals in rosewood, and wheat ears in rosewood, walnut and maple. An unusual feature of the floor design is the arrangement of the wood by tone and hue: the dark saturated tones are used towards the centre, then the colours get softer and paler, ending with dark tones again in the outer border. The texture and grain of each piece of wood has been carefully positioned to achieve the maximum effect from reflected light.

The inlaid floor has been replaced twice: in 1887, a replica was installed when the original floor became very worn, the present floor replaces this 19th century replica which was gutted by fire in 1944. The newly restored floor looks particularly magnificent and striking because one can see the detailed and meticulous craftsmanship required to produce it.

ABOVE: The classical ceiling design in the Throne Room of Maria Feodorovna features a painting entitled 'Ariadne Crowned by Bacchus'.

OPPOSITE: The Throne Room of Maria Feodorovna was also sometimes known as the Picture Hall. The paintings are by Western masters such as David Teniers the Younger, Nicolaes Berchem and Jan Miel.

BELOW: Detail of one of the delicately moulded panels of the ceiling.

One lintel panel depicts huge lobsters in deep relief, creeping out of rocks and weeds and surrounded with delicious fruit and exotic flowers. The other shows a lion peeping out from behind shrubs and a corn sheaf. Both scenes owe more to the imagination of the craftsman than to reality.

The 16 pairs of fluted square Corinthian pilasters break the long extent of wall space into sections and above them is a simple moulded cornice. In 1796-97 Brenna installed marble reliefs into the wall panels. Two high reliefs, featuring episodes from the life of Alexander the Great, are located by the Antechamber door: the first depicts Alexander's father, Philip of Macedonia, greeting his son after Alexander had broken in the horse Bucephalus; the other shows the death of Alexander during one of his many campaigns. Both were executed by Tomazo Solari, a little known 18th century sculptor from Genoa. The wall opposite the windows holds four 17-18th century reliefs of different styles and schools: 'Fight of Putti' by François Duquesnoy, 'Priestess in a chariot' by an unknown master, and two marble medallions after episodes in the Trojan war – 'Paris' rape of Helen' by Giovanni Marchiori, 18th century, and 'Aeneas rescuing his father from burning Troy' by Gian Maria Morlaiter, 18th century. These two medallions were originally intended for the Great Hall of the Chinese Palace, but the oval reliefs by Marie-Anne Collot were installed instead.

The third wall displays a collection of antique reliefs. Over the fireplace is a fragment three feet high which once belonged to the Trajan Memorial and was later transferred to the Arch of Constantine. The relief depicts Emperor Vespasian making an offering, and dates from 701 A.D. The story of its purchase is rather mysterious: the version most commonly believed is that the fragment was uncovered at the Thermae of Titus site, not far from the spot where the Laocoön had been found. In 1769 it was bought by Count Shuvalov for Catherine II from the English sculptor Joseph Nollekens.

The white marble fireplace was added at a much later date during the reign of Nicholas I. To the left of the fireplace is a marble bas-relief entitled 'Shephard', a Roman work from the 1st century A.D. Above it is a relief with two figures, an enlarged model after an antique cameo. The interior of the White Hall was originally also decorated with marble busts, statues, and vases, most of which have now vanished.

In the time of Tsar Paul I Gatchina had four Throne Rooms: two of them for the Emperor, one for his wife Maria Feodorovna and one for the Crown Prince Alexander on the top floor. According to an official statute the Emperor's throne had either eight or three steps, the Empress' Chair of State had one step, and the Crown Prince's throne was placed on a carpet straight on the

ABOVE: The unusual ceiling design has gilded mouldings of Roman legion eagles, winged sphinxes, wreaths, garlands and rosettes against a background of pale pink and pistachio.

LEFT: The Throne Room of Paul I is small, but is one of the most beautifully decorated rooms in the ceremonial suite. The throne once had a canopy of orange velvet with silver thread embroidery, which is currently under restoration.

floor. This statute was strictly observed during Paul's reign, both at Gatchina and at the Mikhailovsky Castle in St Petersburg.

On the west side of the White Hall is the Throne Room of Maria Feodorovna, a square room of 48 sq m which also looks out onto the front parade ground. This room was sometimes called the Picture Hall, for its raspberry silk upholstered walls are all covered with symmetrically hung pictures of carefully

LEFT: The doors and walls in the Throne Room of Paul I are decorated with gilded mouldings. The design of the lintel panels includes cornucopias, sprigs of oak leaves, a mask and a pair of winged dragons.

ABOVE: Detail of one of the door panels.

chosen subjects in gilded frames. These were painted by such Western masters as David Teniers the Younger, Nicolaes Berchem and Jan Miel, among others.

Set within the classical moulding of the ceiling is a painting, 'Ariadne Crowned by Bacchus' which was painted in the post war period. The throne, which was originally set on a podium between the windows, was upholstered with raspberry velvet, under a similar velvet canopy with gold thread embroidery.

The Throne Room of Paul I to the south of the White Hall was once Count Orlov's study. The room is small – only 50 sq m – which is unusual for such an important State room, but Brenna created a special decorative interior to turn it into the highlight of the whole ceremonial suite.

The sumptuous splendour of the room is characteristic of Brenna's interiors. The gilded ceiling mouldings are of Roman legion eagles, winged sphinxes, wreaths, garlands and rosettes against a striking pale pink and pistachio background. The wall panels and doors are lavishly covered with gilded wreaths, ribbons, masks, and urns with flowers. The design of the semi-circular lintel panels includes cornucopias, sprigs of oak leaves, a mask and a pair of winged dragons. The marble fireplace is set with semiprecious stones of different colours.

The floor was designed by Rinaldi and is one of the most intricate in the palace. It uses many unusual varieties of wood: some shapes and borders are in rosewood, 'tobacco' wood (a rare kind of green ebony) and mahogany, while a few details and central inlays are in palm wood and pear wood.

Until 1941 the gorgeous elaborately carved and gilded throne between the windows sat under a canopy of orange velvet with silver thread embroidery. The canopy has become very worn over the years and has not yet been restored.

The walls of the room are hung with valuable tapestries. The Gobelins above the fireplace was woven in the 1770s to the design of Claude Audran III and represents the goddess of fertility Ceres, symbolizing the summer. This tapestry is from the 'Portieres des Dieux' series, which consisted of eight tapestries representing allegories of the seasons and the elements. The side walls are hung with two signed Gobelins 'Asia' and 'Africa' from the workshop of J. Neilsson, from the 'La Tenture des Indes' series, woven in 1780-81 after the designs of François Desportes. All the Gobelins were a gift of Louis XVI to the Grand Duke Paul during his visit to Paris in 1782.

To the west of the Throne Room is the Raspberry Parlour, which is the same size and shape and was again decorated by Brenna. Before 1941 the walls were hung with three Gobelins tapestries from the 'Story of Don Quixote', woven in the 1776-80s after the design of Charles-Antoine Coypel under the supervision of Claude Audran III and Pierre F. Cozette. The central tapestry depicted 'Ladies serving upon Don Quixote'. These were reputed to be the best tapestries from the Royal Gobelins works and were also part of the gift from Louis XVI and Marie Antoinette. These tapestries will soon be reinstated, when the room restoration is complete.

The ceiling is decorated with rosettes set in shallow square coffers, mouldings of imaginary antique musical instruments and a floral scrollwork pattern, all gilded against a pale raspberry background. The doors, with their rich gilded decoration and ornate semi-circular lintel panels, look like triumphant portals. The pilasters set on each side are lavishly decorated with gilded mouldings of wreaths, oak and laurel sprigs, horns of plenty, flower bouquets, ribbons, and foliage. Huge elaborately carved and gilded volutes support the semi-circular arches which frame the paintings over the doors.

The room previously contained the objets d'art made by the Empress Maria Feodorovna herself: a small ivory fountain, a tiny ivory memorial with two bronze lionesses guarding the steps up to a jasper vase (the ormolu handles of the vase were chased as snakes spurting water into it). Another jasper vase was

ABOVE: The ceiling of the Raspberry Parlour has moulded decoration of rosettes set in shallow square coffers, antique musical instruments, and a floral scrollwork border with birds.

RIGHT: The richly ornate doors of the Raspberry Parlour, with mouldings of wreaths, oak and laurel sprigs, horns of plenty, flowers and ribbons.

ABOVE: The ceiling is beautifully moulded with rosettes, decorative bands, acanthus leaves and lion masks.

LEFT: The impressive decor of the Marble Dining Room is reminiscent of Imperial Roman architecture. Behind the balustrade at the far end of the room is a marble statue of Eros with a quiver of arrows.

BELOW: A pair of inlaid and polished wood doors in the Marble Dining Room, showing the detailed ormolu ornamentation.

engraved: "Marie Ce 24 Avr 1793" – an Easter present to Paul I.

On the east side of the Throne Room, the impressive decor of the Marble Dining Room is reminiscent of Imperial Roman architecture. It is likely that Brenna created this room by combining two of Rinaldi's chambers into a single huge hall. The walls are lined with sixteen fluted Corinthian columns of white Carrara marble, set in pairs along the sides but with single columns to emphasize the corners of the room. Stucco mouldings of a triple laurel wreath decorate the narrow space between the double columns, which also holds lights shaped as hunting horns. The wider panels between the pairs of columns have a more elaborate stucco composition of musical instruments, gardening tools, a flower basket and a wreath. A low marble balustrade decorated with urns runs across one end of the room, dividing off an area which was originally used as a buffet or serving space. Behind the balustrade there is a marble statue of Eros with a quiver of arrows.

At the opposite end of the room is a fireplace set between two richly decorated pairs of doors. It has an unusual bronze relief of putti painting a portrait of a farm boy. The boy has typical Russian features and wears the clothing of the period, which indicates that it was made in Russia. A mirror in a gesso frame is set above the fireplace, above it is an elegant medallion supported by two dogs which depicts dancing maenads. There was also once a white porcelain medallion with a profile portrait of Paul I, set in an ormolu relief decorated with cherubs – a copy of an agate cameo made by Maria Feodorovna – but this medallion was stolen during the occupation.

The doors are decorated with detailed ormolu ornamentation, against a background of inlaid and polished wood. Over the doors and windows are sculptured reliefs of episodes from Greek mythology – the Danaids, Apollo, maenads in procession – which form a broad frieze around the room.

In the pre-war period, the ceiling had two paintings: 'Apollo and Muses' by a Russian artist, Gavrila Lokhov, and 'Bacchus and Ariadne' by an unknown 18th century Italian painter. Both canvases were stolen during the occupation, so when restoration work was carried out they were replaced by paintings of the Italian school taken from storage in the Russian Museum. The ceiling is beautifully moulded with rosettes, decorative bands, acanthus leaves and lion masks, and it also has two unusual panels with panthers in relief on either side of the central painting. The cornice design includes a repeating initial M for Maria Feodorovna, the wife of Paul. The floor has a relatively simple geometrical pattern composed of light coloured woods, such as maple, apple wood and birch, combined with dark mahogany, walnut and rosewood.

ABOVE: The panels between the columns of the Marble Dining Room have an elaborate stucco design of musical instruments, gardening tools, a flower basket and a wreath. The lights between the columns are shaped as hunting horns.

Brenna remained among the most outstanding architects in Russia until he left in 1802. In 1796 Catherine II died, and Gatchina immediately became a royal town. The Senate, the Synod and the Court were even transferred there for a few weeks from St Petersburg on the whim of the recent recluse at Gatchina who had now become Tsar Paul I, Emperor of all the Russias.

Few of Paul's successors were fond of Gatchina. Nicholas I made Gatchina his headquarters during seasonal manoeuvres at neighboring Krasnoye Selo. Under him both square tower wings were redesigned and new state apartments were built in the Arsenal for the royal family, although the main building remained intact as a historic monument. In 1857 Alexander II transferred the ceremonial Tsar's Hunt from Peterhof to the forests of Gatchina.

Alexander III lived a simple life style at Gatchina, although about 5,000 employees were still required to look after the estate. The Tsar, who had became Emperor after his father's assassination by populists, chose Gatchina as a long term residence because security was easier to enforce there.

After the 1917 overthrow the palace was turned into a museum, but some of its superb collections were sold by the Soviet Government or were stolen. Even so, when visitors of the period saw what remained, they were amazed at the sumptuous grandeur of the interiors.

World War II and the German occupation of the area from September 1941 to January 1944 caused tragic losses and incurable wounds. Before the German army retreated they set the palace on fire and the trees of the park were ruthlessly cut down. When Russian soldiers arrived to liberate Gatchina, they read the following on the walls: "Hier sind wir gewesen, hier commen wir nicht mehr. Wenn Ivan kommt, ist alles leer." (We have been here, we will never return. When Ivan comes, everything will be empty) Although the solid walls and a few fragments of the decor withstood the destruction, life and beauty seemed to have abandoned the palace for ever....

In 1944 most of the debris was cleared, provisional roofing was built and holes were patched up to make the building habitable. The palace was then assigned to the military and they caused even more destruction. Due to the unceasing efforts of a few individuals – not the Soviet government but real guardians of culture – the military personnel were forced to move out and restoration work was finally begun in 1977. At present only six rooms are completed, work on another 6-7 rooms is in full swing.

The elegant beauty of the newly restored rooms reminds us of the words of Stanislaus Poniatovsky in the 18th century: "Pavlovsk was only a small treasure in comparison with Gatchina, where everything was grandeur."

CHAPTER FOUR

The Tauride Palace

The Tauride Palace is one of the earliest purely NeoClassical buildings in Russia. It was built for Prince Grigory Potyomkin, who was created Prince of Tauris and given the title 'Serene Highness' by Catherine II in 1787 after his success in winning the Crimea (Tauris) from the Tatar Khans, subjects of the Turks.

In 1787, as Viceroy of the newly-annexed land, Potyomkin invited the Empress to visit the area. She took with her all the foreign ambassadors and distinguished visitors from Europe and each foreign envoy was assigned his own palace in Kiev, completely furnished down to the porcelain and wine. Potyomkin staged a fairyland along the whole route – less for Catherine herself than for her foreign guests. To the sound of fanfares, orchestras playing and a cannon salute, eighty huge replica Roman galleys, richly embellished and gilded, slid down the Dnepr river. Guests admired the passing scenery, watching peasants in their Sunday best dancing and praising Catherine's wisdom and beauty; in the distance they could see groves of trees and neat prosperous towns. What they did not know was that Potyomkin had devised portable settlements to camouflage the misery of the people from the Empress and her foreign visitors. The groves and towns were all painted on boards and as soon as the flotilla had passed the imitation trees were uprooted and the illusory villages were rapidly packed and everything was taken miles ahead and reassembled along the route. The trip was a succession of feasts, public welcomes and deputations from all kinds of nomads and local people. The term 'Potyomkin villages' became a synonym for a hoax. Later a string of new cities did spring up in the region – Azov, Nikolayev, Odessa, Sevastopol.

The tour was the culmination of Catherine's glorious reign and of their devotion. Catherine had a talent for surrounding herself with gifted statesmen and warriors. Among these 'Catherine's Eagles' the most prominent was the magnificent Grigory Potyomkin: her incomparable lover, shrewd foreign minister and close advisor, recklessly bold Commander in Chief – and probably her husband. Potyomkin gave distinction to her reign and much of Catherine's greatness was due to this extraordinary, resourceful, masculine, contradictory Russian giant.

Grigory Potyomkin, the son of a colonel from Smolensk, was a brilliant student at the university in Moscow but was soon expelled for not attending his studies. He joined the Horse Guards in St Petersburg and, serving as a sergeant in the Guards, he attracted the attention of Catherine at the time of her coup. At her request he once boldly did one of his famous impersonations, imitating her strong German accent. Onlookers were horrified, but the Empress laughed

PREVIOUS PAGE: The Tauride Palace, one of the earliest NeoClassical buildings in Russia, was the largest palace in Europe when it was built.

LEFT: The dome of the Cupola Hall has a curved false ceiling which was painted by Giovanni Scotti in trompe l'oeil grisaille to give the effect of coffering.

and from that day on he was firmly fixed in her memory. The Orlov brothers tried to stop their mutual admiration developing any further; they once challenged Potyomkin to a game of billiards as an excuse to start a brawl, as a result of which he lost an eye.

In 1774 Catherine broke with Grigory Orlov and fell in love, totally and madly, with her 'Cyclops' – who was ten years younger than she was. She was fascinated with his knowledge of Greek, Latin, French, and German, his phenomenal memory and the audacity of his projects. She wrote, "He is the greatest, the most bizarre and most entertaining of eccentrics."

Even after their passionate sexual relationship cooled Grigory did not lose his influence. He chose her subsequent lovers who all obeyed him with the exception of the last, Platon Zubov. Potyomkin remained both a leader in Russia and a dominant figure in Europe until his death. He was a man of extraordinary contrast, capable of enormous concentrated effort to accomplish a goal and yet indolent or bored when he had attained it, coarse at one time and gallant at another. Catherine showered him with honours, estates, and decorations – according to the historian Walishewsky, Catherine spent 92,500,000 rubles on her many lovers, of which Potyomkin received 50,000,000. He was an

LEFT: View through the octagonal Cupola Hall to the Colonnade Hall. One of the unique features of the Tauride Palace was its open perspective, as originally the columns on the far side of the Colonnade Hall were also open giving an uninterrupted vista into the Winter Garden.

RIGHT: The four oval stucco medallions in the pendentives of the dome depict the liberal arts. The decorative foliage surrounds were added much later by Scotti.

incredibly wealthy man who owned estates worth nine million rubles and 35,000 serfs, and yet he was constantly in debt. His generosity was legendary and he spent fortunes on presents. It is easy to understand her fascination with this wayward, handsome Russian genius who was larger than life. "Bold mind, bold spirit, bold heart", she called him.

There are two versions of how the Tauride Palace came to be built, the most common is that Catherine ordered it as a gift for Grigory Potyomkin. The other reliable version suggests that in 1783 Potyomkin undertook the construction himself, as a ceremonial building for the Horse Guards regiment. Potyomkin obviously chose the site and commissioned the architect, and probably spent his own money in the hope of selling the palace later to the regiment at a profit. As he was permanently in debt, Catherine paid for the building and then gave it to Potyomkin, commissioning a designer to turn it into a glorious palace. When Grigory was alive the palace was called 'Horse Guards House' or 'Potyomkin's House'; in September 1792, after he died, the Empress ordered that it should be renamed the Tauride Palace.

The site was massive, as the gardens originally ran all the way to the Neva river, but its location was not immediately appealing. In the 1770s the area was

BELOW: The NeoClassical stoves in cream ceramic in the corners of the Cupola Hall feature a raised design of Hercules slaying the Hydra.

ABOVE: View up into the dome. A gigantic gilt bronze chandelier hangs from its centre.

OPPOSITE: View through the double Ionic columns into the Cupola Hall from the Colonnade Hall.

on the outskirts of the capital, surrounded only by fields, muddy roads and barracks for regiments of Horse Guards. The only nearby building to catch the eye of the visitor was Rastrelli's Smolny Convent, with its beautiful cathedral.

The architect for the project, Ivan Starov (1744-1808), was a priest's son born in Moscow and trained at the Academy of Fine Arts in St Petersburg which had been founded in 1757 by Empress Elizabeth. He graduated in 1762 with first class honours and went to France to study under Charles de Wailly. He also travelled in Italy and he did not return to St Petersburg until 1768. His principal creation in St Petersburg was the Holy Trinity church of the Alexander Nevsky Monastery. He also worked as a town planner in the south of Russia, at Nikolayev and Ekaterinoslav (now Dnepropetrovsk), where he became known to Potyomkin. Starov never became one of Catherine's favourite architects, his purely 'Russian style' was not to her taste.

The construction of the palace began in 1783 and continued until 1789, with long interruptions. The main façade is extremely simple and restrained, but in no way severe. The central two-storey block is quitc low – as the windows in the second row are very small – and is topped with a shallow dome. The main portico in the centre has six plain Doric columns supporting a pediment. Single storey galleries on either side terminate in two storey wings, each has a portico with four plain Ionic columns. The daffodil-yellow walls have no ornamentation, the beauty of the façade lies in the simplicity and excellence of its proportions and in the classic balance of components.

The austere exterior contrasts with the rather more lavish interior. The entrance vestibule leads into the Cupola Hall, a large octagonal room that rises to 12 metres – the full height of the palace under the dome. The dome has a curved false ceiling which is smooth but was painted in trompe l'oeil grisaille by Giovanni Scotti to give the effect of coffering. A gigantic gilt bronze chandelier hangs from the centre.

The northern wall was originally designed in the form of a triumphant gate, with two pillars faced in granite and four in jasper and an inscription above saying: "To Catherine the Great". The columns of the eastern and western walls were of white marble and above them were galleries decorated with stucco moulding, which were intended for an orchestra; the galleries were reputed to hold up to three hundred musicians simultaneously. The west gallery held a huge gilded organ so for the sake of symmetry the wall of the east gallery was painted with an organ to match. The organ itself was dismantled in 1803 by Rusca, who also redesigned the area into its present form. In around 1819 Giovanni Scotti altered the interior by adding paintings en grisaille, including a

ABOVE: Detail of the ceiling frieze of griffins, trophies and profiles of antique heroes painted by Giovanni Scotti after the concept of Carlo Rossi.

RIGHT: Starov's instinctive sense for the "poetry of columns" achieved its most successful expression in the breathtaking Colonnade Hall, which is nearly 74.5 metres long.

frieze based on episodes from Homer's 'Iliad' on the eastern and western walls. He also added decorative foliage surrounds to the four oval stucco medallions in the pendentives of the dome. The four NeoClassical stoves in cream ceramic in the corners feature a raised design of Hercules slaying the Hydra. The Cupola Hall was often compared with the Pantheon.

Through the enormous double Ionic columns of the south wall is the stunning Colonnade Hall, also called the Catherine Hall. One of the unique features of the Tauride Palace was its open perspective, as originally the columns on the far side of the Colonnade Hall were also open giving an uninterrupted vista from the entrance vestibule to the enormous Winter Garden at the rear of the building. The oval Colonnade Hall is breathtaking – it is nearly 74.5 metres long and 14.9 metres wide. Such a massive area could comfortably hold five thousand people and after it all other rooms seem dwarfed. It is all in white, with 36 Ionic columns running the whole length of each side in two rows – here Starov's instinctive sense for the "poetry of columns" achieved its most successful expression. At each end of the hall is a double row of windows, the arched top of the lower row and the circular upper row echoing the rounded shapes of the columns.

SPQR

ABOVE: The narrow bands between the wall panels in Catherine's Bedroom are painted with lush garlands of summer flowers.

A frieze en grisaille of griffins, trophies and profiles of the heroes of antiquity runs round the ceiling. The design has been renovated a few times since the end of the 18th century and the original painter is unknown. In 1803 Shcherbakov painted it and in 1819 Giovanni Scotti – under the supervision and after the concept of Carlo Rossi – repainted it again as a long uninterrupted frieze to emphasize the room's colossal size. He also added the six rosettes in the centre of the ceiling. The colours are all subdued and neutral, there is no gold detailing. The motif 'SPQR', signifying 'The Senate and people make one whole', was added to the frieze much later in the State Duma period. Chandeliers of black crystal with clocks and musical devices were bought by Potyomkin for this room, but they were later replaced by a range of similar multi-tiered chandeliers with double eagles which hang in the middle of the hall with smaller versions between the columns – there are 56 in all. The floor was originally inlaid with precious woods.

The famous Winter Garden, which was several times larger than that of the Imperial Winter Palace, had a temple in the centre with a marble statue of Catherine II by Fedot Shubin. It was flooded with daylight through a massive pyramid-shaped glass skylight and filled with exotic plants.

It was in this magnificent setting that Potyomkin gave a grand party in April 1791 to celebrate the capture of Ismail from the Turks. The ball also afforded him an opportunity of showing his gratitude towards his benefactress: twice the Empress had paid his debts and presented the palace back to him. The party was so extraordinary that it eclipsed all the other balls mentioned in contemporary chronicles. A whole month elapsed in preparation: poets and composers produced odes and anthems, and artists of all kinds were constantly employed. Each ballet rehearsal – at which the dancers were people from the highest ranks of society – turned into a feast and hundreds of people worked daily to prepare the banquet.

Whole shops were emptied of their goods; all the available wax for lighting in St Petersburg was purchased for 70,000 rubles and a special courier had to be sent to Moscow for more.

Three thousand guests were invited, all dressed in masquerade costumes. Grigory himself wore a scarlet tailcoat with a collar of black bejewelled lace, his hat was embroidered with so many precious stones that it was too heavy to wear and an aide had to carry it round after him.

Catherine ascended a platform in the centre of the salon to watch the entertainments. Her two grandsons, Alexander and Constantine, performed a ballet with 24 pairs of dancers from the best aristocratic families. All their costumes were covered with jewels estimated to be worth millions of rubles. The brilliant illumination throughout the rooms increased the splendour of the festivity. The most sumptuously decorated room was for the Empress to gamble in: the walls were adorned with the richest Gobelins tapestries, chairs and Turkish divans were specially purchased for 46,000 rubles (the gala introduced Turkish divans into fashion). After an interval an amazing clock, in the shape of a gold elephant ridden by a Persian, gave a signal and a magnificent stage appeared on which were performed two new ballets and a comedy. In the main room dinner was served for six hundred people, with another thirty three tables laid out in the adjoining rooms, and all the plates and cutlery were of gold or silver. Potyomkin himself served dinner to the Empress.

When the Empress left after midnight, with obvious regret, an Italian cantata sung to organ music was performed in her honour. She expressed her pleasure to Potyomkin and he threw himself at her feet, kissing her hand and bathing it with his tears. Catherine was very moved and also cried.

The party was Potyomkin's farewell. Two months later he left with the army, never to see his palace again. In the south he suffered a reoccurrence of malaria and in October 1791, aged 52, he died in the field on the way to Nikolayev. There was no gold coin to close his one eye and a Cossack offered two copper five kopeck pieces. Catherine was overcome with grief on hearing the bad news. She fainted several times, was all tears and despair and ordered the court into deep mourning.

The palace interior was not completed during Potyomkin's lifetime, the work was only finished in 1795. A real soldier, he preferred living rooms furnished with plain silk or satin rather than elaborate painting. To cancel his colossal debts (over two million rubles), Catherine took the palace with all its furnishings into the Imperial treasury at a price of 2,611,144 rubles and 1.5 kopecks. She ordered architects and artists such as Feodor Danilov, Gradizzi and Feodor Volkov to add painted decoration, to install new ceramic stoves and to replace doors with more ornate ones with precious wood inlay. In 1793 she also commissioned Volkov to design a theatre in the east wing, which was decorated by Jacopo Ferrari – his canvas paintings for the area still exist in the Moscow Art Academy. Unfortunately only four of Starov's original plans and hardly any other records of the interiors have survived, so it is impossible to attribute much of the interior decor to any specific artist.

Catherine's Bedroom, Boudoir and Oval Drawing Room in the east wing were renovated, as she had decided to use the Tauride Palace as her private residence in the autumn. It was one of her favourite buildings, not only because of

ABOVE: At the base of each garland of flowers is a painted urn decorated with acanthus leaves.

BELOW: Detail of the white marble fireplace in Catherine the Great's Bedroom. Its delicate design is inlaid in semiprecious stones from the Urals.

LEFT: Catherine the Great's tiny Bedroom is exquisitely decorated. In her day the plain panels in the bed alcove were mirrored and a French window in the opposite wall led into the gardens.

RIGHT: The painted ceiling of the Bedroom, with its pastoral scenes, dates from when Catherine used the room.

BELOW: Detail of one of the ceiling paintings. The subject may appear perfectly innocent to modern eyes, but the image of the goat was heavily symbolic of voluptuousness and sensuality and thus rather risqué at the time.

RIGHT: Catherine's Boudoir is painted a deep rich blue, with wall panel borders featuring fronds of stylized foliage and autumn berries.

BELOW: Detail of one of the wall panel borders.

her strong feelings for Potyomkin but also because it had no stairs.

Catherine's Bedroom is exquisite and cosy, although in her day the alcove was decorated with mirrors where there are now plain panels. The painted ceiling is authentic, with its two pastoral scenes featuring shepherds, a maiden and a goat. These may appear perfectly innocent to modern eyes, but the image of the goat was heavily symbolic of voluptuousness and sexuality and thus rather risqué at the time. The rock crystal chandelier is also authentic. The white marble fireplace is truly exquisite, with its delicate design of a dancing nymph, sweeping foliage, berries and wild flowers inlaid in semiprecious stones from the Urals.

The walls are panelled and the narrow bands set between the panels are painted with lush garlands of summer flowers. The columns and pilasters on either side of the bed alcove are bright blue scagliola. The floors in all these rooms are original, they were never removed from the palace as were the precious and beautiful floors in other areas. The bedroom once had a secret passage which connected it to Grigory's rooms.

In Catherine's Boudoir the colour blue prevails. Typical antique Classical motifs are used in the ceiling, frieze and wall painting. The wall panel borders are painted with fronds of stylized and flowing foliage with flowers and autumn berries. The crystal chandelier, with its typically Russian cobalt blue central stem, dates from the late 18th century. The fireplace is set across the corner of the room, with a massive mirror above it.

The Oval Drawing Room has a rich and colourful painted ceiling, with medallions depicting a goddess and a cherub playing music, painting, and sculpting against a romantic landscape. The painted pilasters and wall panels show a variety of field flowers and wild berries.

ABOVE: Detail of the beautiful floor from one of Catherine's rooms. The floors throughout her suite of rooms are all original, as the area was sealed up when she died on the orders of her son Paul I.

One other surprising original interior is the tiny Snuff Box Room near the north west corner of main block. The walls and ceiling still have their elaborate painted decoration, with colourful bands of summer flowers on the walls and a delicate fan in the ceiling decorated with winged figures. Perhaps it escaped destruction because it was so tiny, and it has never been redecorated as for years it has been used as a cleaner's store.

Potyomkin's semicircular Study or Divan Room in the east wing has beautiful painted walls and ceiling, but this was done after his death by Ferrari when Alexander I used these rooms. The chandelier, with its cobalt blue glass central stem, is of the 18th century but it is impossible to know if this was installed when Potyomkin was alive.

Next door his aide's room is an unusual deep blue, with painted borders and ceiling in a variety of rich colours – again by Ferrari. The wall panels have hanging rods set at the top, which suggest that the room was originally hung with tapestries or large pictures. The gilt bronze chandelier has a three-headed eagle at the top, but only two of the heads are ever visible at any one time.

The Arabesque Room is currently under restoration. The magnificent white ceramic stoves have raised decoration featuring oak leaves and acorns. The circular medallion on the base shows a nymph and cherub studying a sheet of music. Of the decor in the remainder of the palace, hardly anything remains.

The Tauride Palace was once one of the wonders of Europe. Its scale may owe much to Starov's training in Paris, but nowhere except in Russia could the grandeur of his design have found fulfillment in actual execution. Its total area of 650,700 sq m made it the largest palace in Europe and its design influenced

ABOVE: The Snuff Box room was used as a Divan Room by the Dowager Empress Maria Feodorovna. Divans were first introduced to Russia by Potyomkin in the Tauride Place and were blamed for "ruining the morals of the Russian people and making them lazy and indolent".

architectural development in even the most distant Russian provinces; for forty years many smaller versions of the central block with plain walls, simple six column portico and a low dome appeared in wood as well as stuccoed masonry. The popularity of the design showed just how directly Starov's masterpiece appealed to the cultivated Russian taste of the period.

After Catherine died in 1796, Emperor Paul I ordered the brutal desecration of the building – he hated all the places associated with her lovers. All the treasures, furniture and lovely inlaid floors were removed and transferred to his Mikhailovsky Castle. In 1799 he quartered a Life Guard Horse regiment in the Tauride Palace and the Colonnade Hall and Cupola Hall were turned into stables. From 1801 to May 1802 the Life Guard Hussars used the building as their barracks. Paul ordered his mother's rooms to be blocked up as if they never existed – he felt they had been defiled by Potyomkin – thus they survived the destruction and remain authentic.

Catherine's grandson, Emperor Alexander I, put an end to further damage and decay. Many of the treasures were returned and the Italian architect Luigi Rusca (1758-1822) was commissioned to restore the building, although it had been so badly damaged that he practically had to re-build it. In 1802-4, to

ABOVE LEFT: The magnificent white ceramic stoves in the Arabesque Room have raised decoration of oak leaves and acorns.

ABOVE RIGHT: Detail of the front panel of the stove, which shows a nymph and cherub with a sheet of music.

factories and water tanks began to obstruct the river approach. The famous Winter Garden was used in 1899 for the International Fair in gardening.

The final destruction of the palace occurred in 1905, when the building was remodelled to accommodate the State Duma which had been set up as part of the constitutional reform. The architect Shestov supervised the rapid dismantling of the vast Winter Garden and it was rebuilt as an assembly room. A wall

ABOVE: The delicate fan design and elaborate painting on the ceiling of Dowager Empress Maria Feodorovna's former bedroom shows elements of Empire style combined with former purely classical features. The decoration was done by Luigi Rusca and Giovanni Scotti.

ABOVE: The central rosette also uses a fan motif, combined with garlands of flowers and flowing ribbons. The open design of the gilt bronze chandelier makes it look light and insubstantial, in perfect harmony with the delicate and detailed painting.

was built to close the open colonnade between the Winter Garden and the Colonnade Hall and the palace lost its unique vista. Many of the 18th century interiors were also lost: the Gotlissovaya Sitting Room to the east of the Cupola Hall, the Chinese Hall, and the theatre in the east wing were turned into ordinary rooms for utilitarian purposes.

For dozens of years the Communist Party School held refresher courses in the Palace. It is currently the headquarters for the parliamentary assemblies on a CIS and international level.

ABOVE: This unusual chandelier dates from around 1770-80 and is in a room previously used as a dining room by the Dowager Empress Maria Feodorovna. Its central stem is of white porcelain with delicate gold arabesque painting - Russian chandeliers of this type typically had coloured glass stems. Porcelain was first made in Russia in 1744 in the Imperial porcelain factory, but was not in mass production until 1752.

CHAPTER FIVE

The Yelagin Island Palace

THE YELAGIN ISLAND PALACE, one of the most enchanting examples of the Russian Empire style, is situated on the utmost northern island of the Neva river delta. The island changed hands many times from the time of Peter the Great onwards: the most notable owners were Peter the Great's associates Shaffirov and Yaguzhinsky and Catherine II's powerful favourite Grigory Potyomkin – who occasionally entertained the Empress there. Yet the name that is most associated with the island – and from which comes its name – is Ivan Yelagin, a nobleman and Marshal of the Court under Catherine II, who bought the island from Potyomkin.

Yelagin owned the island for a long period and he built a simple two storey stone house, with services in separate buildings around it. He was very hospitable and ordered his butler to offer a meal to every visitor – this was something that Russian aristocracy often did at the time. Under Yelagin the island was full of entertainment and laughter and was nicknamed 'merry island.' On festival days musicians played in the gardens, with jugglers, comedians, and rope dancers to entertain the crowds, and fireworks in the evening. People came in their Sunday best to stroll along the shady paths, under ancient oak trees which were said to have been planted by the Swedes in the 17th century. Visitors delighted in the overwhelming sunsets over the Bay of Finland in the fairy tale 'white nights' period in May and June, when the sun drops below the horizon for only a very short time each day.

In front of the palace is a field known as Butter Meadow, named after the festival of Maslenitsa or Butter Week. This celebration was held there every year in old Russia to bid farewell to winter. Yelagin treated everyone to piping hot pancakes and the gardens were filled with dancing bears, swings, jesters and masques. Artificial hills, or 'montagne russe', of 30-40 feet were constructed in ice and snow, for people to slide and toboggan down.

After Yelagin died the island changed hands several times and in 1807 was sold to Count G.V. Orlov. In 1817 the island was bought by Tsar Alexander I from the Orlov family for 350,000 rubles. He planned to construct a summer residence there for his mother, the elderly Dowager Empress Maria Feodorovna. On the night her husband was murdered in March 1801 Maria had followed the example of Catherine II and tried to proclaim herself Empress, on the grounds that she had been crowned with Paul. It took Alexander several days to persuade her to relinquish her reckless claim. For some time afterwards, whenever her son came to visit, Maria would place a casket between them containing the bloodstained nightshirt that Paul was wearing on the day of the murder as a silent reproach. By 1817 the relationship between mother and son

ABOVE: The doors in the Oval Hall are masterpieces of Russian craftsmanship, made of Karelian birchwood with carved and gilded ornamentation. On the reverse side of these doors the central panels feature a nymph holding a lyre, which represents the goddess Terpsichore.

ABOVE RIGHT: An elaborate frieze of caryatids and bas-relief panels, by Vasili Demut-Malinovsky, runs round the Oval Hall at high level.

PREVIOUS PAGE: The Yelagin Island Palace is positioned on a raised terrace, with a wonderful view towards the Spit where the sun hardly sets in summer.

was much improved and he promised her a new palace nearer the city, as she was beginning to find the long trips to Gatchina and her beloved Pavlovsk very tiring.

The young Carlo Rossi (1775-1849) was commissioned to redesign the old buildings, which were rough and heavy and had been badly neglected during the course of the 1812 war. He was also to incorporate a new palace into the existing gardens. This was Rossi's first important commission in St Petersburg, although his name was already familiar in Moscow where he had restored several mansions belonging to the aristocracy after they had been gutted by fire during Napoleon's invasion. Now, however, the architect had to prove his talent, and demonstrate his knowledge and distinctive artistic taste, to the autocratic customers of the capital.

Rossi, the illegitimate son of an Italian ballerina, was born in Naples. He arrived in Russia as a small boy with his mother and choreographer step-father and grew up in St Petersburg. Later he went to study for two years at the Academy in Florence, where he learnt the principles of Classicism. He eventually originated the majestic Russian Empire style, and his creative achievements marked the height of the development of Russian Classic architecture.

Rossi's name is world famous, he designed a number of monumental Neo-Classical buildings, grand administrative buildings and magnificent palaces. St Petersburg is inconceivable without his principle masterpieces – the grand sweep of the General Staff Building facing the Winter Palace, the Senate and the Holy Synod, the Mikhailovsky Palace (now The Russian Museum) and the Alexandrine Theatre. Rossi always paid attention to the area around his buildings as well, redesigning the façades of the streets leading to them and placing them in elegant squares. Rossi's work made St Petersburg into the grandest and most beautiful capital in Europe, and marked a heyday in Russian urban planning.

Amongst all these grand buildings, the small Yelagin Island Palace holds its place. Although it only has eleven rooms on the ceremonial floor and was meant as an intimate home, it is one of the finest remaining examples in St Petersburg of Rossi's interior decorative style.

Rossi began work at Yelagin in 1818 by pulling down nearly all the structures on the site, although the old palace, a stone greenhouse, and a pavilion near the granite pier retained their foundations and some lower walls. The island had always been rather marshy and prone to floods but with the gardener Joseph Bush Jnr – the son of the creator of the glorious parks at Tsarskoye Selo – Rossi managed to produce a wonderful palace and garden ensemble. The functional stables and kitchens, the hothouses and follies, were all set in landscaped grounds, while the palace itself was positioned on a raised terrace where it could be clearly seen and was safe from the danger of floods. This solution required a great deal of money: an estimate came to 1,587,632 rubles, while the cost of reconstructing the palace alone was put at 741,747 rubles. The construction work took a total of four years.

The front façade of the main palace has a Classical central portico with six columns, and two flanking porticoes with pediments. The building is decorated with a richly detailed cornice and a beautifully moulded frieze. The exterior is painted an unusual greyish colour, with columns, cornice and mouldings picked out in white. The cast iron grilles, Corinthian column bases, and fifty standard lamps along the front terrace were manufactured at a local foundry. The two carriage ramps which sweep up towards the main entrance on either side of the front façade are marked with huge metal balls. The wide staircase from the ramp up to the raised terrace is guarded by two white lions – a particular feature of Rossi's work. These lions were designed after the two bronze

ABOVE: Intricate detailing on the massive gilded bronze chandelier makes it appear light and delicate. It was made at Schreibers, the famous bronzemakers in St Petersburg.

ABOVE: Detail of the brightly coloured ornamental border of the ceiling in the Raspberry Drawing Room.

BELOW: The former exquisite and fanciful floor patterns of the 18th century were no longer in fashion, but the detailed geometric floors designed by Rossi still look richly magnificent.

lions by Andrei Voronikhin for the Lower Park Cascade at Peterhof. They look down a panoramic vista towards the Spit, to the horizon where the sun hardly sets in early summer. This has been a popular spot with the local residents of St Petersburg during the long summer evenings for over 200 years.

Inside the palace, the State Rooms for balls and receptions on the ground floor are Classical in design and feature the very best workmanship. The living rooms, of smaller size and simpler decoration, were originally situated on the first floor and the top floor housed the family church of St Nicholas, the Miracle Worker.

The central area of the building is occupied by the magnificent Oval Hall, a perfectly proportioned two storey room which runs almost the full depth of the building and extends out in a curved bay from the rear façade. The walls are faced with white scagliola with greyish veining and are decorated with sixteen Ionic pilasters. Above the pilasters is a rich frieze with elaborate caryatids, which was executed by Vasili Demut-Malinovsky. He also made the original model for the bas-reliefs inserted between the caryatids, which feature beautiful maidens decorating antique lamps with flower garlands. The ornamental figure reliefs between the columns and above the doors are also by Demut-Malinovsky.

The ceiling of the Oval Hall is flat, but was painted en grisaille by the artist Barnabo Medici to give the impression of a cupola with coffers and rosettes.

The massive gilded bronze chandelier which hangs in the centre of the hall was made to a design by the sculptor Stephan Pimenov. Natural light floods into the hall through a double row of windows and is reflected by the niched mirrors symmetrically placed on the opposite wall. French windows in the centre of the bay lead to the rear terrace, which overlooks the Nevka river. The steps down into the garden are decorated with four colossal vases of white Carrara marble decorated with bas-reliefs of Triton and Nereids.

ABOVE: The Raspberry Drawing Room has four doors, two of which are false and included only for the sake of symmetry. The floors were made by the parquet makers of Okhta village, which was famous for its superb traditional craftsmanship in wood.

ABOVE: The elegant bronze chandeliers were made by Schreibers in St Petersburg.

OPPOSITE: The north facing Dining Room has windows round three walls and the golden-yellow and white colour scheme is not accidental - even on the gloomiest days the room is bright.

BELOW: Detail of a sphinx from the ceiling design by Giovanni Scotti.

From the Oval Hall doors lead to the Gala Vestibule, at the front of the building, and to the sitting rooms on either side. The doors themselves are masterpieces of Russian craftsmanship, made of Karelian birchwood with carved and gilded ornamentation. The central panel on the reverse of one set features a nymph holding a lyre, which represents the goddess Terpsichore ascending to heaven after she had disclosed her secret magic arts to the human race. The geometric design of the floors is constructed in local types of wood: pine, birch, and oak. The original furniture of Karelian birchwood was commissioned from Baumans, who were the best cabinet makers in St Petersburg, and was upholstered in yellow striped satin.

To the north of the Oval Hall is the Raspberry Drawing Room for ladies, named after the colour of the silk used to cover the walls and furniture. The original wallcovering was paper in raspberry pink patterned with golden rosettes and framed with gilded fillets. This was replaced with silk damask in the 19th century, and the wallcovering in the room at present is a copy of this. The wall surface is divided with narrow vertical panels of scagliola, painted in oil with an intricate arabesque pattern and stylized foliage, flowers, masks, dancing cupids and characters playing flutes. The ceiling was painted by Giovanni Scotti and depicts a brightly coloured ornamental border of triumphant gods in chariots, surrounded with nymphs and cupids dancing and playing music. An elegant bronze chandelier hangs from the centre of the ceiling.

The original curtains and upholstery were of yellow silk with raspberry pink flowers, designed to add a bright note to the decor and to contrast with the furniture of mahogany and gilded bronze. Two pedestals of black marble and two of yellow marble held candelabra and porcelain vases with a gold tinted crimson background. The floors were made by the parquet makers of Okhta village, now a part of St Petersburg, which was famous for superb traditional craftsmanship in wood. The former exquisite and fanciful floor patterns of the 18th century which reflected the ceiling design were no longer in fashion. The classicists preferred plain lines, clear contours, strong geometric forms and exact symmetry. Floors designed by Rossi still looked richly magnificent – they were highly detailed and divided strictly into chevrons, circles, squares, and polygons, with the colour and the texture of the wood enhancing the geometric designs.

The mahogany doors were made by the master craftsman Grosse and are decorated with gilded carving in linden wood. Linden is very close grained and smooth, and is easy to carve, which makes it particularly suitable for this type of very detailed work. The Raspberry Drawing Room has four symmetrically

ABOVE: Ceiling detail from the Blue Drawing Room, showing one of the dancing nymphs painted by Giovanni Scotti.

placed doors, but only one fireplace. Two of the doors are false – included only for the sake of symmetry in the decor. The beauty and the variety in design of the different doors in the Yelagin Island Palace is its special glory – in fact its nickname is the 'Palace of Doors'.

The Dining Room at the north end of the enfilade is a long rectangular room with numerous wide windows along three of its walls. The remaining wall has two pairs of doors, and mirrors which reflect the light from the windows. The walls are faced in creamy scagliola, with pilasters in yellow scagliola. The pilasters are square in section, gently tapering from top to bottom, with capitals of sculptured heads wearing Ionic spiral headdresses. They were executed by Demut-Malinovsky, as was the elaborate white Roman nail motif in the yellow marble frieze. The frieze and the ornamentation of the lintel panels over the doors were also by Demut-Malinovsky.

The doors are decorated with delicately detailed carving in wood, lacquered in yellow. The elegant bronze chandeliers and wall sconces were made by Schrcibers in St Petersburg. The ceiling and coving were painted by Giovanni Scotti with colourful scenes of Bacchus feasting – between each scene is a sphinx and there are candelabra painted in each corner. The bacchanalian scenes were replaced with new paintings in the 1840s. The original Karelian birchwood furniture was upholstered in lemon yellow plush with an embossed design, while curtains were in yellow taffeta. The golden-yellow and white colour scheme in this north facing room was not accidental – even on the gloomiest days the Dining Room looks bright and attractive.

On the south side of the Oval Hall is the Blue Drawing Room for gentlemen, with walls covered in blue taffeta. This room is particularly remarkable for the fireplaces, which were made by the sculptor Stefano Maderno in black Italian marble with white veining. They have huge mirrors above them in carved and gilded frames, which are carefully placed to reflect back and forth to create an endless succession of rooms.

The doors in this room are of poplar wood and have rich borders by Grosse, decorated with carved and gilded geometric designs and garlands, wreaths, vignettes and masks. The paintings over the doors are flanked by two caryatids on tiny corbels, which appear to support the skillfully modelled and gilded cornice. The ceiling is again painted by Giovanni Scotti, with dancing girls around the centre and various scenes en grisaille round the edges. The floor design is typical of Rossi, who liked inlaid floors to have a broad frieze of dark oak with a meander design in lighter wood.

At the south end of the main enfilade is the Porcelain Room, which must be the most beautiful in the palace. The walls have no columns or pilasters – they are of scagliola, perfectly smooth and richly painted. The beautifully detailed oil painting on both walls and ceiling was done by the famous artist Antonio Vighi after Rossi's designs. The ceiling has a delicate design of flower garlands, with chariots driven by cherubs and drawn by flying moths. In the painted frieze there are cupids with bows and arrows, holding garlands and laughing and playing. The wall panels, which are framed with gilded and painted borders of masks, blossoming roses and lilacs, feature twelve Graces. Vighi depicted the Graces either in groups of two or three in a swirl of dance, or posing gracefully alone. Vighi's assignment, as detailed in a contract dated March 1822, was "to paint in gold arabesque, to look like French porcelain". He fulfilled the commission brilliantly, as the room does indeed look as if it is made of delicate porcelain. The doors are decorated with gilded cast bronze, formed into delicate sprigs and tiny blossoming rose buds.

The Bedroom next door was originally upholstered in white taffeta draped in folds, with festooned draperies of silvery satin woven with gold-orange flowers and white swans. The poplar wood furniture was again from Baumans. The bed, positioned on a raised poplar platform, was covered by a rug from the Imperial tapestry works. The Bedroom had special acoustics – before going to bed the Empress, who was becoming rather deaf, always liked to have a book read to her. She never complained about not being able to hear at Yelagin, as the ceiling was specially domed to reflect the sound. This room has not yet been fully restored.

The last room in the south wing was a Boudoir, which had finely gilded bronze ornamentation. Again this has not yet been restored.

The decoration of the interior of the Yelagin Island Palace was distinctive in that it used entirely Russian materials and artwork produced by Russian companies – in contrast with the Mikhailovsky Palace which was built during the same period using some imported materials. Both before and during the reign of Catherine II top quality furniture and decorative materials were nearly all imported – mainly from France. By the first quarter of the 19th century Russian manufacturers had became strong and independent, capable of producing art objects of quality and good design. People began to believe that a nation who had defeated Napoleon was certainly capable of creating its own decorative art, and should not be buying it from Europe. The idea of using mainly Russian masters on the interiors and to place orders for most of the interior items with Russian manufacturers – to turn the Yelagin Island Palace into a kind of national showpiece – was enthusiastically welcomed by both Rossi and society.

ABOVE: A pair of doors in the Porcelain Room. The beauty and variety of the doors in Yelagin give it its nickname of the 'Palace of Doors'.

ABOVE: The panels of the ceiling have a design of cherubs driving chariots which are drawn by flying moths.

ABOVE RIGHT: Detail of two Graces on one of the wall panels.

LEFT: Each of the wall panels in the exquisite Porcelain Room has a different painting of the Graces, by Antonio Vighi. The panels are bordered with delicate garlands of roses and lilacs on either side of a gilded band of masks and stylized foliage.

The desire to avoid foreign help reflected the general spirit and the growth of a feeling of national independence. It is worth mentioning that Rossi's assistants, although they had foreign names, were descendants of the original immigrants and had long before become native Russians. They formed the team which was traditionally employed to work on his other projects.

The aged Empress Maria was perfectly at home in her Yelagin Island residence. Here she could relax and regain her long lost sense of peace in a tranquil atmosphere, devoid of gloomy memories of her murdered husband or the hardships of the 1812 war. The earlier mistrust between Maria and Alexander was long forgotten and there was a growing sense of confidence and cordiality between them. Alexander even entrusted his mother with State secrets that he would not confide to his own brothers.

The fresh air of Yelagin Island was always inviting, and she enjoyed the beautiful views of the Nevka river (a branch of the Neva), with its crowds of people in gaily decorated boats with singers and musicians. Just across the river stood Alexander's palace, and scattered in the vicinity were the lovely villas of the rich aristocrats Laval and Zinoviev and the 'Ma Folie' dacha owned by Dimitri Naryshkin – whose beautiful wife had once been the Tsar's mistress and considered as the uncrowned Russian Queen.

LEFT: The ceiling of the Bedroom is slightly domed which gives the room its excellent acoustics. The Dowager Empress Maria Feodorovna, who had become rather deaf, liked to have a book read to her before bed.

After Maria Feodorovna died in 1828 the palace was carefully maintained as Romanov private property, but was not often inhabited. Successive emperors used it occasionally to house distinguished guests and it survived almost in its original form for over 120 years – until World War II.

In September 1941, the siege of Leningrad began. In early 1942 the palace was shelled, and a wall crashed into the main hallway causing a fire. The palace continued to burn as people were too exhausted by hunger to extinguish the flames. Precious ceilings, doors and reliefs perished in the heat and smoke, and for a long period after the war the palace was exposed to the elements. A few fragments of the interior decor, much distorted in colour by the flames, survived and were used as the basis on which to restore the palace's vanished beauty. Fortunately all the original blue-prints and drawings by Rossi survived, so it has been possible to restore most of the palace to its former splendour.

The Yelagin Island Palace opened the door to fame and glory for Carlo Rossi. He more than proved his unique abilities; that he could create beautiful buildings in a very short space of time, that he had the talent to design everything from a construction detail to a door handle. Rossi, more than any other architect of this period, was inspired by the glory of ancient Rome and he gave St Petersburg much of its Classical grandeur. He died in 1849 and in 1912 Igor Grabar, the art historian and painter, wrote of him: "Rossi was gone, the last fanatic of the Classic idea, the genuine keeper of the Antique behests."

The Maryinsky Palace

THE MARYINSKY PALACE is unique in St Petersburg in that it is the only palace which was built for a daughter of the Imperial family. The grand duchesses were expected to marry foreign princes, so their destiny was to leave Russia and spend their lives as part of other European dynasties, but in the 19th century the Grand Duchess Maria Nikolayevna firmly refused to marry if it meant leaving Russia and changing her religion.

When Maria eventually fell in love and married Duke Maximilian-Eugene-Joseph-August-Napoleon of Leuchtenberg, nephew of the King of Bavaria, against tradition he came to live with her in St Petersburg. Their marriage caused quite a commotion, not only in Russia where the groom's father was best remembered for destroying Moscow 26 years earlier with the retreating French army, but also in Bavaria where the Catholic house was in dismay that Maximilian's children were to be brought up in the Russian Orthodox faith.

On her engagement Tsar Nicholas I decided to present Maria with her own palace. He chose a site in the centre of St Petersburg by St Isaac's Square, on the banks of the Moika river near the Blue Bridge. In the second half of the 18th century the land had been occupied by the huge palace of Count Chernyshev, a well known statesman in the reign of Catherine II, who died in 1797. In 1816 the Treasury bought his palace and by 1838 the building was being used as a school for military cadets. The existing site was enlarged by the purchase of three private houses nearby.

The Tsar wanted his daughter's palace to be the most beautiful in St Petersburg, but also to be a comfortable home. The design had to incorporate the top technical and engineering solutions of the day, to pioneer new ideas in layout and design, and to use modern building materials and methods to ensure its durability and cut construction costs. On top of all this, the overall design of the building had to take into account all the fashionable new trends in architecture.

The late 1830-1840s marked a considerable decline in Classicism in Russian architecture, as a new trend – Eclecticism – began to develop. Eclecticism called for the application of a variety of different historical styles to the same building – particularly in the interiors, where they were harmoniously combined to create a richness of design. In 1838 the draft project for the Maryinsky was offered to Carlo Rossi, the most outstanding exponent of the Russian Empire style. At 63 years old, however, Rossi was too set in his ways to create the type of building required and the project was eventually awarded to a relative newcomer – Andrei Stakenschneider (1802-1865).

Stakenschneider was a young and talented Russian architect, of German descent, who had already begun to make a name for himself by designing and

PREVIOUS PAGE: The Maryinsky Palace, set in the Classical ensemble of St Isaac's Square, is the only palace in St Petersburg which was built for a daughter of the Imperial family.

redecorating a few fine buildings in St Petersburg and its outskirts. In 1834 he had been awarded the title of Academician, and his diligence, versatile knowledge and exquisite taste meant that he was becoming well known in his profession and popular with wealthy clients. The Maryinsky Palace was his first really important commission in St Petersburg. His capacity for work was prodigious: throughout the five years he was supervising construction on the Maryinsky site he was simultaneously engaged in building several palaces and villas for other members of the Imperial family on the southern coast of the Gulf of Finland, near Peterhof and Strelna.

The initial designs of the Moika site residence were taken for the Emperor's approval in December 1838. An order from the Tsar dated March 1st to Prince Volkonsky (a minister of the Imperial Court), stated that the construction works were to be supervised by Stakenschneider in person and that the required money would be allotted by the Crown Lands Department. The construction cost was estimated at only 700,000 rubles, although materials such as marble, zinc and cast iron – all relatively expensive at the time – were to be used in the work.

The official foundation ceremony took place in autumn 1839. Work proceeded at a fast pace because some of the basement and walls from the earlier Chernyshev building were used, so that by the end of 1840 the building work was almost finished except for two pediments and the central attic floor.

By carefully placing the building on its asymmetrical site between two streets, Stakenschneider succeeded in making the palace appear to be a part of the almost complete Classical ensemble of St Isaac's Square – the dominant feature of which was the half-finished St Isaac's Cathedral. In 1842-1844 the Blue Bridge in front of the palace was widened from 41m to 97.3m to correspond to the front façade of the Maryinsky, and thus the building seemed even more an integral part of the square. In gaining such a wide approach and grand outlook, the Maryinsky Palace became one of the most imposing palaces in St Petersburg – second only to the Winter Palace of the Emperor himself.

To the ordinary people of St Petersburg the swift growth of the Maryinsky – directly opposite St Isaac's on which work continued for forty years – must have seemed fantastic. In less than a year and a half there appeared a monumental residence with an amazing façade of over 100 metres, and three floors reaching to a height of nearly 20 metres. In plan the palace is unusually asymmetrical; the right wing is not only much shorter than the left wing, but is also at an oblique angle to the main façade due to the line of Voznessensky Avenue.

The front façade of the Maryinsky is in traditional Russian Classical style,

although at the time this was just beginning to go out of fashion. The central section and the side wings are set slightly forward, the mass of the ground floor is emphasized with diamond rustication, and the two upper storeys are lined with Corinthian columns and pilasters. The central section has a high attic storey decorated with six volutes, with a double headed eagle in relief in the centre which gives an imposing Imperial feel to the façade.

Sandstone, a construction material which had recently become popular, was used for decorative features on the front façade such as columns, pilasters, corbels, cornices and window architraves. The stone was brought from Narva (now Estonia) to St Petersburg by water – down the Luga river and along the Gulf of Finland. Sandstone is an attractive yellow-grey in colour, relatively strong but easy to cut and polish.

The main entrance has a projecting portico with wide central steps and two sweeping side ramps. The two end arches frame antique style standard lamps and above the portico there is a wide balcony with a decorative balustrade and six Italianate cast iron vases, covered in stucco to match the façade.

The Entrance Hall on the ground floor has columns of pink Tivdian marble from Karelia and the floor was originally of granite laid in a herringbone pattern. The walls of the arcade were painted with arabesques. To the left of the hallway marble animals on metal plinths guarded the base of the main stairs, flanked on either side by two huge bronze lamps. This area was substantially redecorated at the end of the 19th century, and only the pink marble columns and pilasters remain.

From this area the wide and imposing Grand Staircase leads up to a half landing, where it then opens out into two stairways leading to the first floor. The metal staircase balustrades are painted very dark green, highlighted with bright gilded bronze. The intricate design of the balustrade is in rich contrast to the simple white walls, which are only decorated with niches containing statues of antique warriors and wall brackets supporting classical busts. The busts are believed to depict Paris and the three goddesses who claimed the golden apple – Juno, Venus and Minerva. Throughout the palace there are representations of Venus, and it is certain that this was not coincidental. Maria, the favourite daughter of the Tsar and a very beautiful woman, identified strongly with the goddess of love and beauty. The detailed vault mouldings are punctuated with medallion paintings depicting scenes from the Trojan War.

In the centre of the first floor is the Rotunda, a wonderfully light and airy double height space which reaches up 17 metres into a glass skylight. The ceiling, with moulded decoration against a gilded background, is unusual struc-

LEFT: The Entrance Hall, which was substantially redecorated at the end of the 19th century, leads into the Grand Staircase.

ABOVE: The metal staircase balustrade is painted very dark green, highlighted with bright gilded bronze. The original green paint had been covered with subsequent decoration and was only discovered during the restoration work carried out in the late 1970s.

LEFT: View of the Grand Staircase from the half landing, looking towards the first floor. The elaborate stair balustrade is in rich contrast to the simple white walls.

RIGHT: The letters of Maria's name are formed into an intricate gilded motif, which is used throughout the palace.

turally: the stone dome rests on the walls at only four points. Gilded bronze chandeliers hang between the 32 columns which encircle the room in two tiers. The frieze at second floor level has a design of pairs of gilded griffins, each pair holding a lyre.

Behind the Rotunda is the Square Room, a two-storey area bright with natural light through a large glass skylight. The Square Room is only separated from the Rotunda by the open gallery at second floor level and the columns above and below. The height of the Square Room and its skylight give the area a feeling of lightness and space although it has no windows. The walls are painted with murals in Pompeian style, a particularly popular motif of the Renaissance revival. The decorative surrounds to the wall panels feature mythical characters, birds and animals in Grotesque style, and arabesques and plant forms. The walls and the landscape paintings above the doorways were painted in tempera on plaster by Drollinger, who also did the wall medallions in oil on

ABOVE: Detail of the central marquetry floor design in the Rotunda.

LEFT: The frieze at second floor level around the Rotunda has a design of pairs of gilded griffins, each pair holding a lyre. Above this delicate border is the light and elegant open ironwork of the gallery balustrade.

ABOVE: Looking up to the ceiling decoration around the central glass skylight.

canvas. The ceiling is magnificently coffered and richly painted – again in tempera on plaster by Drollinger. Grand torchéres of bronze and porcelain, made at the Alexander Imperial porcelain works after a drawing by Stakenschneider, originally stood in the four corners of the room.

On the opposite side of the Rotunda three pairs of doors lead to the magnificent Gala Reception Room, which is set directly above the Entrance Hall. The room looks out across the square towards St Isaac's Cathedral and has five windows in two rows, the lower ones opening onto the balcony over the entrance portico. The beautiful inlaid parquet floor is designed in a wide variety of precious woods.

The high Italianate ceiling, which is finely gilded and painted, is plaster on a metal mesh and was the first example of its kind on such a scale. Nine huge bas-reliefs above the cornice feature episodes from Homer's 'Iliad', after the design of the famous English NeoClassical sculptor, John Flaxman (1755-1826). They alternate with eight enormous alto-reliefs of ancient armour.

The dark red marble Corinthian pilasters are in fine contrast to the elaborate white Carrara marble fireplaces. The dark red was deliberately chosen to echo the colours of the red granite colonnade of St Isaac's across the square. The fireplace frieze depicts idyllic scenes from peasant life in relief, while the side panels are elaborately carved into detailed trees. The rather Germanic feel of

ABOVE: One of the huge bas-reliefs above the cornice depicting scenes from Homers 'Iliad'.

LEFT; Side panel of the fireplace showing a bird in the tree, on the other side the bird is sitting on a nest to symbolize that Maria had now started a family.

ABOVE: Panel detail from one of the seven rosewood doors. Each of the main panels features a god, goddess or warrior in flowing pink and blue robes, driving a chariot. Each chariot is pulled by a different animal, including lions, swans, deer, peacocks and horses.

RIGHT: The Gala Reception Room, showing the pilasters of dark red marble and the intricately designed parquet floor.

the design is attributed to the influence of Maria's mother, Empress Alexandra, who was Princess Charlotte of Prussia by birth.

The highlight of the room is undoubtedly the exquisite doors of highly polished rosewood, which are elaborately inlaid with ivory, mother of pearl and copper. The design features flowers, mythical characters driving chariots, helmeted warriors with swords, griffins, birds and delicate arabesques. The door handle is a gilded bronze bird's claw holding a wooden globe – the globe moves freely within the claw but cannot be removed. This Stakenschneider design became very popular as a motif in jewellery. There are seven doors in all, three of them were commissioned in Munich in 1842, the others were made to match by Russian craftsmen.

Originally the focal point of the room was an enormous agate vase on a porphyry plinth, above which one could see the top of the water fountain in the Winter Garden on the far side of the Rotunda and Square Room.

Unfortunately the Winter Garden was remodelled after the State Council

RIGHT; A section of the richly decorated ceiling panels, painted in tempera on plaster by Drollinger.

LEFT: A view of the Square Room. Murals in Pompeian style were a particularly popular motif of the Renaissance revival.

BELOW: Detail of the painted decoration of the Square Room.

took over the building in 1884-5. It originally stretched through all three storeys, with numerous grottoes and cascades and a central fountain spurting a jet of water 8 metres into the air. Among the pathways laid with marble mosaics, palm trees and other unusual plants grew in 30 marble flower boxes and exotic birds strutted and preened. Another fountain of thin streams of water, decorated with shells, was called the Fountain of Tears. It was designed after the Bakhchisarai fountain in the Crimea and was the prototype for the fountains in the Pavilion Hall of the Small Hermitage. This spacious garden, with its arched pillars and eight columns, received abundant daylight through over 1,000 glass panels. Decorative busts were set in niches and a marble staircase led to the upper gallery, where there were many more rare plants. Anna Tiutcheva, a lady-in-waiting whom Grand Duchess Maria received in her garden in 1853, thought it "A real mirage of spring amidst the January frost".

To the west of the Square Room is the Oval Parlour, while to the east are the Concert Hall, Library and Pompeii Gallery. The Concert Hall has two rows of windows with NeoGreek details and was famous for a sculptured frieze with paintings on the theme of Mars and Venus. These scenes were painted by Antonio Vighi, an elderly master whose skillful brush had decorated many palaces and villas in St Petersburg and its surrounding areas. This painting was his last commission – the artist died while working on it.

The ceiling is moulded and coffered and its three huge chandeliers, with matching wall lights, were made in 1842 in the Imperial glass factory. Unfortunately the original marble fireplace, with its two caryatids holding musical instruments, was dismantled in 1945 and the caryatids were replaced with two columns.

The position of the Library, within the gala suite of rooms as if it were open

LEFT: Detail of the wall painting in the Pompeii Gallery.

to everybody, was unusual for the period. Libraries were normally located in private areas, near the master's study for his personal use. Duke Maximilian was one of the best educated princes in Europe and became well-known as a scientist throughout Russia. His library contained over 50,000 volumes and was decorated with nine stylized cameos of distinguished philosophers, scholars and poets through the ages. The Library had a doorway direct into the family Dining Room. This compact placing of the gala rooms along the palace axis, interconnected with numerous doors, meant the palace interior could be turned into a single entity, comfortable and spacious enough to accommodate many guests.

The private rooms are in a different style. They are situated in the west wing of the palace and consist of two suites, one for the Grand Duchess and one for the Duke. The rooms at the front overlooking St Isaac's Square were used by the Duke of Leuchtenberg, and his Study and Sitting Room were decorated in simple good taste. These rooms contained a wonderful collection of paintings by Western masters which had been acquired by the Duke's father, Eugene Beauharnais. The Duke himself collected rare minerals and antique weapons.

The private rooms of Grand Duchess Maria were designed by Stakenschneider around various historical styles. Her Study, and the neighbouring Reception Room, are decorated in a restrained Florentine Renaissance style. The pillars and pilasters feature delicate moulded ornamentation highlighted in gold, and miniature medallions. Similar, but larger, medallions are set in the frieze. The coffered ceiling is a very unusual design, painted in bright colours by Drollinger. There are two fireplaces in the room, one of them beautifully decorated with detailed scenes in mosaic. Nestor Kukolnick, a playwright who was among the first visitors to the palace, wrote of rich furniture – the antique cabinets in particular – and pictures by Ivan Aivazovsky, Timothei Neff and Tyranov, among others.

The Bedroom is entirely different. The walls are painted a rich dark tone and the ceiling is decorated with paintings of nymphs and the sleeping Venus. The letters of Maria's name are formed into an intricate gilded motif which is set at the apex of the heavily decorated scagliola arch over the bed alcove. The fireplace is in a particularly handsome and unusual black marble veined with orange. The motif of Maria's name in smaller characters is also shown above the mantelpiece and on the curtain pelmets.

After all these rich colours, the elegant Bathroom with its restrained white scagliola walls comes as a surprise. The octagonal room is set round with eight caryatids, dressed as antique handmaidens ready to attend Venus at her bath. There are four different figures, each repeated twice; one holds a looking glass, one a jewellery box, one a cup and the final one holds the magic girdle of Venus. The ceiling is painted with eight different scenes of 'The Toilette of Venus', with cherubs and Graces assisting the goddess as she bathes.

The Boudoir was heavily decorated in Louis XV style and resembled a wedding candy box. Kukolnick wrote: "In this boudoir a la Pompadour, one doesn't feel like arguing: it makes one feel fine, merry, grand. The focal point is hard to choose – all around there are mirrors, there is elaborate gilded woodcarving, there is a damask of silky splendour, there are various pictures a la Watteau. It is a dazzling mixture of elegant bric-a-brac in its infinite multitude."

ABOVE: Maria's Study was decorated in a restrained Florentine style and the unusual ceiling was painted by Drollinger.

BELOW: Detail of the ceiling design and frieze in Maria's Study. The delicate moulded ornamentation of the pillars and pilasters is set against a gold background, with miniature medallions set within the design.

RIGHT: The Reception Room, which is almost devoid of natural daylight, seems very light because of the soft tones of the scagliola and the delicate white mouldings. The doors are flanked with unusual three quarter length columns, which are fluted at the base and have gilded mouldings of arabesques, birds and floral garlands above.

The little Corner Study originally had paintings by Antonio Correggio, Guido Reni, Carlo Dolchi and other Western masters and was connected to the Duke's suite by a hearing tube. When fully furnished Grand Duchess Maria's rooms, lavishly decorated with damask and silk upholstery, mirrors and beautiful furniture of the highest craftsmanship, must have looked stunning. Not much of the original decor of these rooms remains, but the area is now under restoration.

Right at the top of the palace, in the attic storey above the Gala Reception Room, was the family Church of St. Nicholas (Nikolskaya). "This minute place is astonishing in its sumptuousness, gracefulness and splendour," the 'Petersburg Leaflet' (Listok) assured its readers in 1885. The Church was originally lit through the ceiling and the walls were plain white. The wooden iconostasis was

ABOVE: Maria's name used as a gilded motif on the apex of the arch over the bed alcove.

LEFT: Maria's Bedroom was originally decorated in rich, dark tones. The ceiling has paintings of nymphs and the sleeping Venus - Maria, the favourite daughter of the Tsar and a very beautiful woman, strongly identified with the goddess of love and beauty.

BELOW: The fireplace in the Bedroom is of a particularly unusual black marble, veined with orange.

also painted white, with rich gilding on the holy gates and carvings. The icons of the holy gates and the iconostasis were painted by the academician Duzzi. Maria later decided to have the walls and ceiling painted and the work was commissioned to Prince Grigory Gagarin, Vice-president of the Academy of the Arts, in 1856-1860. He designed the biblical scenes and also had the altar area rebuilt. The subjects of the paintings are not accidental: they all feature Jesus' grace to a woman – 'Healing by touch', 'Healing of the widow's son at Nain', 'Jesus and an adulteress'. The murals were done after Gagarin's drawings by Troshchinsky in a special mastic of his own make. This "paint" of resinous components was made to a special recipe with secret ingredients; it dried out in a few minutes, had no bad smell, did not go off and was damp proof.

"The panicadilo of the church is most exquisite," a contemporary remembered. "It consists of a cross-shaped candlestick which has icon-lamp mats instead of candles, creating a wonderfully favourable religious atmosphere." Under the Bolsheviks the walls of the Church were plastered in plain white and only 15% of the authentic paintings survived. It has only recently been fully restored to its former glory.

The Oratory did not have a complete iconostasis, only its central part – the holy gates. The icons on the holy gates were after the mosaic icons at St Sophia's in Kiev: 'Annunciation', 'Evangelists', 'Divine Teachers', and 'Deacons'. Among the best icons were 'Trinity' in the Greek style, 'The Vladimir Mother of God', and a wooden triptych of local saints. The stairs up to the church were decorated by the best professors of the Academy of Art.

Contemporary reports also noted the beauty of the Catholic church, built on the ground floor for the Duke of Leuchtenberg. This was remarkable for a stained glass panel depicting the Mother of God and two saints: Maximilian and Eugene. This panel was made at the Royal factory in Munich in 1842.

The children's rooms were also situated on the ground floor. "The rooms are of an extraordinary size", wrote Illustration magazine in 1845. "Particularly large is the Recreation Hall off the Winter Garden."

Contemporaries of Stakenschneider appreciated his technical skills, and reports of the day spoke proudly of new technical feats – particularly when these were ahead of progress in France, at that time the accepted leader in architectural technology. Stakenschneider used fireproof construction elements extensively: metal overhead covers on metal struts and bars, metal netting in ceilings to support the plaster. Fire resistance was of overriding concern to Tsar Nicholas because of the sudden and awful fire which had destroyed much of the Winter Palace in December 1837. For three days the fire had raged through the building, and even the Tsar and his brother the Grand Duke Michael had personally taken part in efforts to quench the flames. So in 1845 reports of the Maryinsky Palace emphasized: "In the whole palace everything is made of stone and metal, except for the floors... ".

Stakenschneider also came up with a clever solution to the other main requirement of his illustrious client: that of creating a comfortable home. To begin with he situated the service and guest rooms facing out onto the street, while living rooms were placed inside the palace, away from the noise of rattling carriages and street pedlars' calls. Although on the inside of the building, the private rooms were still well lit and sunny as they looked out onto spacious inner courtyards.

Secondly, the stairs were well planned and carefully positioned. Grand Duchess Maria probably suffered either from varicose veins or from some sort of bone disease, and by the end of her life she had become rather less mobile.

LEFT: The elegant Bathroom is set round with eight caryatids, dressed as antique handmaidens ready to attend Venus at her bath. The walls are of plain white scagliola.

RIGHT: Detail of one of the caryatids, holding a cup. The Ionic capital incorporated in the design also acts as her head-dress.

Any sort of illness in the Imperial family was kept very quiet, and both father and daughter undoubtedly urged Stakenschneider to come up with solutions to protect the secret.

A unique ramp was designed and installed in the right wing, connecting all three floors away from the main rooms. The ramp was used for wheel chairs and prams, and for walking up and down to "avoid shortness of breath". The oval ramp room receives natural light through a large skylight in the ceiling, the light reaches down through the open centre of the ramp to the lower spirals. The balustrade and rails are constructed in cast iron and originally the slopes were asphalted, but this was later replaced with parquet flooring. The ramp was the only one of its kind in a private residence in St Petersburg – perhaps the only one of its kind in all Russia. Not long afterwards mahogany hydraulic and pneumatic lifters were introduced, the prototype of modern lifts.

Outside the garden frontage was provided with an additional ramp reaching up to first floor level: "...a wide alley runs through the garden towards the private entrances to allow carriages to approach. One of the entrances is furnished with a ramp reaching to the first floor, thus allowing a light coach to come straight to it", a witness wrote in 1845 in the 'St Petersburg Chronicle' (Vedomosti). This exterior ramp is also described in archive records, although after Maria's death it was dismantled. For his technical achievements on this project alone Stakenschneider was appointed a Professor of the Art Academy, before his plans had even been put into practice.

The interiors of the palace were finished by the end of 1844. Up until this point Maria, her husband, and three children had lived in the Vorontsov Palace, waiting for the completion of their own residence. The new palace was finally handed over in 1845, and was named the Maryinsky by special Imperial decree. "In early 1845, the Maria palace was opened for curious visitors," wrote Kukolnick, "Rooms were thronged with crowds." Contemporary reports of the interior praised its elegance and virtuosity.

In all Stakenschneider not only met the functional requirements in a masterly fashion, developed unique engineering and architectural solutions, and managed to consider both changes in style and the personal whims of the Emperor, he also managed to create a splendid artistic atmosphere which pleased the Grand Duchess. This was quite an achievement, particularly as the Emperor was known to be rather fussy and the Duke of Leuchtenberg, Presi-

RIGHT: The family Church of St Nicholas, which has been recently restored to its former glory. The biblical scenes were designed by Prince Grigory Gagarin.

LEFT: This unique ramp was used for wheelchairs, prams and "to avoid shortness of breath" and connects all three floors of the palace away from the main rooms.

dent of the Academy of Art, also acted as a strict supervisor on the construction site. The Maryinsky Palace made Stakenschneider famous. It established him on his path to success and until his death in 1865 he remained the most popular architect of the Imperial family.

After Grand Duchess Maria's death in 1876, three of her sons by the Duke of Leuchtenberg lived in the palace with their families. By 1884 the family palace had been sold to the Treasury for 3,000,000 rubles to clear some of the family's mounting debts. The palace retained its name of Maryinsky, but now housed the Imperial Council, as well as the cabinet of ministers and other offices. Its interior was not radically changed, although it was refurnished and fitted out for its new function by the architect Peterson. In 1907, however, the Winter Garden was sacrificed to make a meeting hall.

After the revolution the palace housed many different institutions. The siege of Leningrad during World War II caused a great deal of damage and considerable restoration and repair work has been carried out since. In 1945 the Maryinsky became the headquarters of the Executive Committee of the Leningrad City Soviet and now serves in effect as the St Petersburg town hall.

CHAPTER
SEVEN

Grand Duke Nicholas' Palace

IN SPRING 1891 the whole of St Petersburg was agog at the scandal surrounding the sorrowful events in the Imperial family. At Alupka in the Crimea, Grand Duke Nicholas Nikolayevich Snr had died at the age of sixty. His widow, who lived in Kiev, refused to attend the funeral. She also refused to pay homage to the dead when the funeral catafalque taking his body for burial in the St. Peter & Paul Cathedral in St Petersburg came via Kiev on its route from the south.

Tall, strong and very handsome – but some people said rather stupid – Grand Duke Nicholas was an incredible womanizer (as nearly all the Romanovs were). "He loved all women except for his wife", a contemporary wrote, and he did not change even in the very last hour of his life. Although not divorced from his wife, the Grand Duke had developed a permanent relationship with Yekaterina Chislova, a dancer from the Krasnoye Selo theatre. She was an unrivalled partner to the famous Felix Kshessinsky in the Polish mazurka. He was quite open about the affair and had a daughter and two sons by Yekaterina, who was a commoner. He arranged a change of class into the gentry for his mistress and the illegitimate children, who all took the surname Nikolayev.

Grand Duke Nicholas Nikolayevich Snr was the third son of Emperor Nicholas I and his wife Alexandra. He made his career in the army – on the day he was born he was appointed an honorary colonel in the Life Guard Lancers and enlisted in a Life Guard Sappers battalion and as an adult he showed a special interest in military engineering. When Alexander II entrusted all the key State posts to his brothers, Nicholas was appointed Commander of the St Petersburg military region. Eventually he received the ranks of Fieldmarshal-General, Inspector-General of Cavalry and Inspector-General of Engineering forces. The epitome of the Grand Duke's career was during the war against Turkey in 1877-1878, when he was appointed Commander-in-Chief of the Russian Armies in the principal European theatre – although his reputation as a strategist was very low.

Grand Duke Nicholas waited longer than any other grand duke for his own palace, for it took nearly ten years to complete. In 1851, when he attained his full legal age, a contest was announced to find the best design. The eminent architect Nicholas Benois was ready to submit plans and drawings but, despite the fact that the contest term was not over, construction works were commissioned to Andrei Stakenschneider (1802-1865). August Lange and Karl Tsygler were appointed as assistant architects.

RIGHT: The main façade of Grand Duke Nicholas' Palace blends Rococo ornamentation with elements of the Italian Renaissance.

The site selected was in Annunciation Square, in the once neglected outskirts of St Petersburg which previously had only held the insignificant buildings of the docks and a rope factory. By the 1830-40s, however, the area had turned into a lively and fashionable district; nearby was the English Embankment, a favourite promenade for high society. In November 1850 the first permanent bridge across the Neva river was opened in the vicinity, thereby turning the area into a prestigious and costly suburb. The Crown Lands Department owned a substantial parcel of land there, which was allocated to the palace. Stakenschneider's design envisaged the construction of a palace, a manège (riding school), stables and a servant's block, in a total of 20,000 sq m.

Signing up the contracts lasted a year and the foundation ceremony for the Grand Duke's residence took place on May 21, 1853. In 1854 the Crimean War broke out and financing of the project was suspended; work only resumed in 1856, when three million rubles were allotted to build the palace. By that time Nicholas had started a family.

In December 1855, for diplomatic reasons, he unwillingly married Princess Alexandra of Oldenburg – his cousin once removed who was known in Russia as Grand Duchess Alexandra Petrovna. She was not beautiful, but her purity, sincerity and pleasant manner meant that she received a great deal of sympathy. She converted to the Orthodox Russian church and became extremely pious. They had two sons – Nicholas, born in 1856 (who also had a prominent military career as Commander of the Russian Armies in 1914-15) and Peter, born in 1864.

In December 1861, the palace was inaugurated and consecrated. The building is set back slightly into the site to allow it to be viewed from the relatively small square. The plan is a rectangular, with two wings projecting forward from the front façade and three wings projecting back from the garden front. All the rear rooms are arranged around the two inner courtyards, which provide an abundance of light.

The main façade was designed in the rather old fashioned 18th century U shape, blending Rococo ornamentation with elements of the Italian Renaissance. The paved courtyard in front of the building is surrounded with fancy iron railings on a red granite base. The central main entrance has a portico, with four grey granite columns and a balcony above with elaborate ironwork featuring the initials "N" and "A" and double-headed eagles.

Each storey has a projecting cornice and is lined with columns or pilasters. The ground floor has a rusticated stucco finish and Ionic pilasters, its rectangular windows have decorative bas-reliefs above and massive corbels with wreaths

TOP: This corridor on the first floor has a very unusual ceiling with a series of small domes.

ABOVE: Massive double corbels beneath the stairs, with moulded ornamentation of foliage, are after Stakenschneider's drawing.

OPPOSITE: The grand and imposing Entrance Hall has a gallery at first floor level which runs round the entire area. Sixteen grey granite columns support the elaborate stucco vaulting.

ABOVE: Detail of the ceiling in the Church of Our Lady of Sorrow, which was destroyed in 1925 and is currently being restored.

beneath. The tall first floor has Corinthian half columns and pilasters and huge arched windows. The windows at the front of each wing have small balconies with delicate railings. Beneath the windows the terracotta panels moulded in relief were executed by the sculptor David Jensen. The low second floor has a double cornice above Ionic pilasters and was once topped with an Imperial eagle. The garden front faces east and its central wing contains the Church.

This exterior is considered to be the most inconsistent, heavy and simplified of Stakenschneider's creations. The architect is believed to have implemented the original design as approved by Emperor Nicholas I in 1853 before he died, which incorporating the Tsar's personal preferences. The main client, Grand Duke Nicholas, had little knowledge of architecture and had agreed to anything his father suggested.

The interior is in splendid contrast to the design of the exterior. It is light, comfortable, dignified and consistent. The enormous Entrance Hall with its main staircase is grand and imposing, with sweeping stairs, grey granite pillars and elaborate moulded stucco ceiling. The main stairway rises to a half landing and then continues up to finish in front of the Church doors. From each end of the half landing another two stairways ascend in the opposite direction towards the ceremonial rooms at the front of the building. At first floor level a gallery runs round the area with a colonnade of 16 grey granite pillars which support elaborate stucco ceiling vaulting. Above the panelled and polished wood doors – with their distinctive Stakenschneider bird's claw handles – are moulded stucco panels. Marble is used everywhere; supplies were plentiful as St Isaac's construction works had finally come to an end and there were plenty of left-overs. The stairwell was originally hung with 17 specially commissioned paintings by Nicholas Tikhobrazov.

The location of the Church of Our Lady of Sorrow is unique: it is the only family church in all the residences of the grand dukes which is accommodated on the main staircase. The design was chosen by Grand Duke Nicholas, he wanted a replica of the ancient dilapidated church of Our Saviour of Mercy in the Rostov the Great monastery. In 1850 Nicholas had visited the town of Rostov the Great and liked the strict Byzantine style of the church near the Metropolitan's cell, with its high solea podium and expressive ancient wall painting. Construction of the Church commenced in 1853 and it was completed in 1861. Professor Ludwig Thiersch from Munich was commissioned in 1860 to paint wall frescoes after copies taken from the Rostov church. His paintings on Portland plaster were applied in three coats, using special paint containing "melted glass" (siliceous binder). The four Evangelists in the cupola were painted in oils by the Russian artist Ksenofontov.

The Church was divided into separate areas: the solea with nine oak steps leading up to it, a box for Grand Duchess Alexandra, a family area in the south choir and a place for choristers in the north choir. In 1872 a Sacristy in imitation of the Cave of Jesus in Jerusalem, in which to keep relics from the Holy Land, was built by the architect Kharlamov.

The first floor contains the private apartments, the ceremonial rooms and domestic quarters. The most impressive part of the whole building was the enfilade of ceremonial rooms stretching along the front of the building, which consists of five grand rooms.

The rectangular White Parlour at the south end of the suite of ceremonial rooms is divided into three areas by two elaborate arches supported by caryatids; beneath the caryatids is a panel with either musical instruments or an easel with brushes. Smaller caryatids decorate the two white marble fireplaces. The caryatids and the Rococo moulding on the frieze and coved ceiling are by Jensen, while the original paintings over the doors were by Tikhobrazov. This room was used for small receptions and charity bazaars. The decorative repertoire is very restrained and muted, there is no rich glow of gold. Stakenschneider's chosen medium in this palace was moulded stucco work and he used it in almost every part of the building.

To the east of the White Parlour, overlooking the southern inner courtyard, is the Family Dining Room. It has a wonderful profusion of Rococo moulding by Jensen, with a prevailing motif of game, fish, wild life and plants. The floor is in a herring-bone design, with floral motifs in the door carving and pine wall panelling – all painted white. The fine carving of the mantelpiece features birds and animals. Again there is no flamboyant colour in this room.

Every day at twelve noon promptly, Nicholas entered the room for lunch. He started it with a small shot of vodka, saying: "Ein, zwei, drei, Peter komm herein! Gott erhalte mich!" His fat head waiter, Mangold, a retired Prussian sergeant, was a wonderful cook and rather reminiscent of Figaro in both speech and walk. When serving courses he liked to suggest which piece to take and how to handle it. Lunch included starters (zakuski), four courses and a dessert.

The second room in the suite of ceremonial rooms – the Small or Chinese Drawing Room – had furniture in black. The detailed linden wood carvings on the polished wood doors are tinted black to match, and the door architraves are also black with gold banding. Black marble was used for the fireplaces and the window cills, while the wall panel borders have a raised Chinoiserie geometric design.

In the very centre of the suite is the Gala Reception Room or Rose Drawing Room. The walls are elegantly panelled with delicate stucco moulding in white, which was originally against a background of soft rose pink. The rich bas-relief panels over the doors include cherubs and elaborate floral scrolls and the huge mirrors above the fireplaces have gesso frames in the form of plant stems with sprouting leaves and garlands of flowers. The carving of the white marble fireplaces features a monogram and cherubs. Above the mirrors is a semi circular panel which once held a fresco painting. The ceiling was originally decorated with a canvas entitled 'The Judgement of Paris' painted by the Academician Yasevich in 1861. The rich tones of the inlaid wooden floor look rather too ornate against the now plain white of the walls, but must have looked magnificently sumptuous with the original colour scheme.

The northern end of the enfilade houses the Ballroom and the Banqueting Hall. The spacious high ceilinged Ballroom is flooded with daylight from the double row of windows – six in each tier – in the west wall. Once it was even more light and airy as there were matching windows in the east wall, overlooking one of the inner courtyards, but these were later bricked up. Open galleries in the north, south and east walls each have a colonnade of fluted Composite

ABOVE: Detail of moulded stucco work in the White Parlour.

ABOVE: Detail of one of the caryatids by David Jensen in the White Parlour.

RIGHT: There is no flamboyant colour or rich gold in the Family Dining Room, everything is restrained and muted.

BELOW: The fine carving on the fireplace of the Family Dining Room features birds and animals.

columns; all the columns, pilasters and half-pilasters are faced with scagliola. Three huge chandeliers hang from the ornate moulded ceiling, which has unusual ventilation slots with pierced and gilded bronze covers. Smaller chandeliers hang between the columns of the north and south galleries, in both tiers. Nicholas Nikolayevich was an enthusiastic and inventive dancer and dancing was the principal entertainment at the palace. The best military bands played tirelessly, and specially selected officers of the guard were on hand to invite ladies to dance so that none of them felt neglected. Before each winter season Nicholas made a list of the officers who were reliable dancers and crossed out the names of lazy ones. He did this for his own parties, and also for the Winter Palace balls where he was always in charge of the dance program.

The last room in the ceremonial suite, the Banqueting Hall, is one of the largest rooms in the palace. Twelve caryatids are spaced around the walls, which are decorated with elaborate mouldings featuring fish, game, fruit and vegetables. The door panels, coving and ceiling have moulding on the same theme.

The private apartments of Nicholas consisted of six rooms in German Renaissance style, with a profusion of stucco moulding on both walls and ceiling as well as walnut and oak panelling. There were rich inlaid floors with friezes in precious woods and marble fireplaces with ornate stucco tops reaching to the ceiling. All the rooms were decorated in muted tones - bright colours were avoided. The Academician Schwabbe was commissioned to do 14 portraits in oil of the best of the Grand Duke's horses, for these rooms and the manège. Nicholas' suite of rooms had a private entrance from the street and a hydraulic lifter from the ground floor.

Nicholas' suite of rooms adjoined Alexandra's rooms, which were decorated in a mixture of styles and ran along the southern front overlooking the boulevard. Her Study was a corner room in Italian Renaissance style with a richly painted and moulded ceiling and a white Carrara marble fireplace. Next to it was a small Oratory in Byzantine style and a small Winter Garden. Her Boudoir was in restrained Rococo, with rich moulding on the coved ceiling and silk upholstery. A favourite scene of two cherubs is featured everywhere in the decor.

The ground floor originally accommodated the children, the governess, guest rooms and a spectacular Recreation Hall to the right of the Entrance Hall. In the 1880s the rooms on the ground floor were refurbished by the Academician Bassin, who was then court architect to Nicholas, for his two legitimate sons who were now adults.

The north west area held the German Renaissance style rooms of Grand

ABOVE: Doors in the Small or Chinese Drawing Room, with detailed linden wood carving tinted black to match the original furniture.

Duke Nicholas Jnr, as well as his Turkish Room and the Arsenal. These are now all gone without trace.

The southwest area housed the apartment of Grand Duke Peter, of which only the Moorish Room and a fragment of his Study have survived. The tiny Moorish Room has a beautiful tiled floor decorated with stars and geometric borders. Its carved and painted walls are richly coloured in red, blue and gold, with inscriptions in Arabic around the room. The domed ceiling has a bold raised pattern in blue edged with gold against a red background, a small brass chandelier hangs from its centre. Since 1918 the room has been used as the private office of a trade union official.

In the Study only the rich and ornate ceiling – which is coloured to look like carved oak – remains of the decor. Peter's monogram is incorporated in panels in the coving: a combination of the Russian letters "П" and "Н" for Peter Nikolayevich.

The palace was connected to a manège, which contained three rooms for the staff and for spectators. The decoration was entirely Arabian in style, including the fireplaces. The manège was often used for exhibitions of pure-bred dogs, thorough-bred horses and cattle, as there was no better administrator and expert on cattle breeding, hunting and fishing than Grand Duke Nicholas Snr.

Yet again Stakenschneider came up with technical innovations – this palace was among the first homes in St Petersburg to have running water and sewerage. Its heating system consisted of 70 fireplaces, 15 pneumatic stoves, and a great number of 'Russian' stoves in brick, faced with painted tiles. Lightning rods featured prominently on the 92 chimneys, earthed in the large garden to the east of the building.

Scientists, foreign visitors and the intellectual elite were not often seen in this palace. No-one in the family was able to arrange the kind of elaborate and artistic entertainments that were held at the Marble Palace, the Mikhailovsky Palace or the Maryinsky Palace. Well known people visited to wish members of the family happy birthday, and on their namedays. The guests usually talked about horses – "Stereotype and boredom", a contemporary wrote of the gatherings there.

In 1881 Nicholas' nephew, Alexander III, ascended the throne and resolutely deprived his two uncles of all their influence. The Tsar paid neither particular respect to his uncle Nicholas' abilities, nor did he approve of his mode of life which he believed set a bad example to the younger generation.

Family life in the palace was a failure. Yekaterina Chislova nagged Nicholas to provide for her and their children and he soon became financially embar-

RIGHT: The elegant white stucco work moulding of the Rose Drawing Room was originally set against a background of soft rose pink. The gesso frames to the mirrors are in the form of plant stems with sprouting leaves and garlands of flowers.

LEFT: One of the huge chandeliers in the Ballroom. In the background can be seen one of the galleries with its fluted Composite columns.

LEFT: Detail of the elaborate mouldings in the Banqueting Hall. The designs feature different types of food, decorated with ribbons and garlands.

RIGHT: Bronze chandelier in Grand Duchess Alexandra Petrovna's Boudoir. In the background can be seen her favourite scene of two cherubs, which is used everywhere in the decor.

rassed and had to mortgage the building. In 1881 his wife Alexandra left him for good and went to live in Kiev, where she later became a nun. As his grown up sons continued to live at the palace, Nicholas lived as a private gentleman with Yekaterina's family in a modest house. According to his nephew, Grand Duke Vladimir, Nicholas was waiting for his unfortunate sick wife Alexandra to die, so he could marry Yekaterina. However his mistress died a year before he did and Alexandra outlived him by nine years.

Shortly before his death Nicholas went mad – he was convinced that all women were in love with him. The illness became evident when, at a ballet performance, Nicholas became so aroused that he wanted to make love to all the corps-de-ballet dancers there and then. After this episode the family kept him locked indoors, as he would even try to kiss effeminate looking men. For the last few years of his life, Nicholas' reputation at the Imperial Court was not high and his death did not cause anyone profound grief. On March 1 1892 his court was cancelled.

LEFT: The design of the richly coloured ceiling in Grand Duke Peter's Moorish Room is based on a typical Arabic geometric pattern.

RIGHT: The beautiful Moorish Room is a perfectly scaled down version of an Islamic prayer space.

BELOW: The Arabic inscription beneath the window openings means: There is no God but Allah, the Lord.

The Grand Duke had squandered all his tremendous wealth and his palace was immediately sold to the Ministry of the Imperial Court for 3,816,256 rubles to cancel his massive debts. When his legitimate heirs signed the sale papers in 1894 they received just a few thousand rubles and were left with only some furniture and sentimental things from their family house.

LEFT: Detail of the ceiling in Grand Duke Peter's Study, which is painted to look like oak. The panels on either side of the corner contain Peter's monogram.

The Crown Lands Department did not know what to do with the palace. It was later to accommodate a girls school – named after Grand Duchess Xenia, sister of Nicholas II – for 350 students of middle class background. The architects Stephanits and Teslin provided plans to refurbish the building for classrooms and dormitories. The ceremonial rooms underwent few changes, but the ground and second floor rooms were greatly altered. The private apartments were used by the head mistress and the teachers.

In 1917 Lenin decreed that the palace should be handed over to the local trade unions and it acquired a new name – the Palace of Labour. The remaining valuable items were dispersed and vanished. The best rooms, however, became the offices of the communist trade union officials and were properly maintained if not carefully looked after. Only the Church was deliberately destroyed in 1925 and fitted out for temporary exhibitions and meetings; it is now under the process of restoration. The palace is still the headquarters of the trade union movement.

CHAPTER
EIGHT

GRAND DUKE VLADIMIR'S PALACE

GRAND DUKE VLADIMIR was a key statesman in the reign of the last two Russian Tsars, his brother Alexander III and his nephew Nicholas II. As the third son of Emperor Alexander II and Empress Maria Alexandrovna, Vladimir had little chance of ever attaining the throne but he was a recognized leader amongst other grand dukes and a well-known public figure throughout Russia. He was Commander of the Guards and Chief of the St Petersburg Military District – a post he held from 1881 to 1905 – and from 1872 he was a member of the State Imperial Council and a member of the Council of Ministers. Dozens, if not hundreds, of public and charitable societies sought his benevolence, protection, or his services as their president, and his court rivalled the Grand Court in its glory and magnificence. His palace in St Petersburg has survived almost as it was left by the family at the beginning of the 20th century, because in 1918 – at the order of Lenin – it was assigned as a club for scientists and thus spared any destruction.

The land chosen for the palace, on the Embankment near the Winter Palace in the centre of St Petersburg, had previously been occupied by the house of Count Vorontsov-Dashkov. This had been bought by the Treasury much earlier, and the site had later been enlarged by purchasing the neighbouring house of Madam Karatigina. The proposed project was thoroughly scrutinized by a special committee, who noted the opinion of Lieutenant-General Count Boris Perovsky, the head of the Property Department of the Tsar's Children: "Our finances are far from flourishing, and it is useless and harmful to conceal this fact from His Imperial Majesty's sons." His conviction was that "to live on such a lavish scale, with such a large number of staff and servants as before, is no longer possible." The total construction and furnishing cost of the Vladimir Palace with furniture, draperies, carpets and artwork was 820,000 rubles, as against the 2.5-3 million rubles spent on previous palaces for other grand dukes a mere 10 years before.

The architect appointed to the project was the academician Alexander Rezanov (1817-1887). Rezanov was not well known in St Petersburg as he did very little private work, being busy lecturing at the Academy and working as Chief Architect of the Crown Lands Department. He was also appointed as the head of a committee to study old Russian architecture. He designed the Central Meeting Hall of the Academy of Fine Arts and also participated in the contest to design The Church of the Holy Blood in St Petersburg in 1881, but was not successful. His major buildings are the Cathedral of Christ the Redeemer in Moscow and the palace for Grand Duke Vladimir. The Grand Duke – who was known for his strong national spirit – appointed Rezanov because of his pro-

RIGHT: The north facing front façade of Grand Duke Vladimir's Palace overlooks the Neva river, opposite the Peter and Paul Fortress.

26 26

ABOVE: The carved decoration on the main panel of the first floor doors features a medallion with a letter "B" (V in the Russian alphabet) for Vladimir.

OPPOSITE: Designed in the elaborate French Renaissance style of King François I, the Main Staircase is light and exuberant after the sombre Vestibule.

BELOW: Detail of the unusual grained and gilded plaster background on the wall panels of the first floor.

found knowledge of ancient Russian architecture. Rezanov was responsible for the whole project – although separate engineers were responsible for the construction and some of the furniture was designed by his talented assistant architect Victor Shroeter.

The foundation stone was laid on July 15th, 1867 and Grand Duke Vladimir presented Rezanov with a silver snuff box with his personal monogram to mark the occasion. As soon as the blessing ceremony ended, the works began. The palace was under construction for five years, with 20 boats arriving daily to bring new construction materials and to take away the debris from the site. The palace consists of three structures: the main building, which is built round a central main courtyard; a U shaped service building, directly behind the main building and forming a second courtyard; and a stable block for 36 horses and 40 carriages in the middle of the second courtyard. The main building was newly built, although part of the foundations and some of the rear walls of the previous building on the site were utilized. Its main courtyard has elaborately modelled walls bearing Vladimir's coat of arms, and on one side there is a heavily ornate private family entrance. The service building, which overlooks Millionaire's Row (the street behind the Embankment), was an existing building that was merely refurbished.

The front façade overlooking the river is in Florentine Renaissance style; some of the features are reminiscent of the Palazzo Strozzi and the Palazzo Riccardi in Florence. The ground floor is faced in grey granite, while the brick walls above are finished in stucco and rusticated to match the stonework beneath. The lion masks, 14 coats of arms above the first floor windows and other sculptural details were designed by Nicholas Adt and then cast in huge cement blocks and installed during the masonry works. The river façade has three entrances; the main entrance is emphasized by a projecting portico with a balcony in sandstone. On the balustrade of the balcony are two large bronze griffins by the sculptor Schwarz, which seem to guard the palace.

The three storey palace does not look impressive if viewed from the river – the façade is only 45 metres in length and not quite 24 metres high – but the building is much bigger than it appears as it extends back 195 metres into the site. The exterior has changed very little in the course of a century. The interior features a variety of different decorative styles and to modern eyes it sometimes seems rather overdone. This was typical of interior design of the 1880s, where different styles were deliberately used together to create a rich and opulent effect.

The main entrance opens into a small hall or inner porch, which has pol-

ished granite flooring and a stained glass window from Munich after a drawing by Nicholas Sverchkov. This leads into the bigger Vestibule in French Henri IV style, which has a huge sandstone fireplace and a marble floor. The moulded ceiling is painted in imitation of rosewood, and there are handsome carved oak doors – the overall effect is rather sombre and heavy. There was originally a hydraulic lifter behind matching oak doors, but these now lead to a cloakroom. At the foot of the marble stairs two stuffed brown bears stood to welcome visitors with symbolic trays of bread and salt, but since the scientists took over the building these have been replaced with two huge china vases.

To the west are the private rooms of the Grand Duke and the family entrance led directly into this area from the main courtyard. These private apartments consisted of a front hall, a reception or billiard room in English Gothic style, a sitting room in Greek style, a Byzantine study and a library. A choice collection of Russian paintings by the best contemporary artists of the day – such as Ilya Repin, Ivan Aivazovsky, Feodor Bruni, Vasili Vereshchagin, Ivan Kramskoy, Mikhail Vrubel, Nicholas Sverchkov and Rudolf Frenz – was displayed in these rooms. They are now the administrative area of the Scientist's Club. The private quarters also had a very unusual feature: a 'banya' or sauna in Russian style, with a painted tiled stove. Beneath the sauna a mechanical laundry was housed. These facilities represented an innovative technical achievement for the period, but unfortunately are no longer in existence.

On the east side of the Vestibule there was a state of the art showpiece kitchen, with red copper utensils and a manual lifter for food. Next to this, in the basement, was an enormous area for wine cellars and food storage which was included in the design at the express wish of the Grand Duke. Vladimir Alexandrovich was a famous gourmet both in Russia and throughout Europe; he produced a recipe book based entirely on the food he had personally tried and enjoyed. Today the archive records which record the wine ordered by the Vladimirs seem absolutely astonishing: there are thousands of bottles listed, of hundreds of different types of wine. Also stored in this area were the amazing traditional Christmas gifts from the Ural Cossack regiments. As soon as the winter sleigh tracks were established, a convoy with a Cossack sergeant and a few men would bring four to six small barrels of black caviar and five to six prime sturgeons to St Petersburg. In those days sturgeons of around 120 kgs in weight and up to 3.5 metres long were occasionally caught in the Yenissey river and the rivers of the Urals. To preserve the massive fish for their journey to St Petersburg, water was poured over them in the freezing air until they were deep frozen. Vladimir presented the sergeant with a gold watch, while the Cos-

RIGHT: The Drawing Room, which was decorated in Louis XVI style, originally had a colour scheme of blue and white. Most of the furniture in the palace is original, but many items have been moved from room to room over the years.

sacks received 50 rubles each.

After the rather plain and sombre Vestibule, the lightness and exuberance of the Main Staircase is even more stunning. Designed in the elaborate French Renaissance style of King François I, the staircase starts from the Vestibule and leads straight up to a half landing. There the original staircase turns back on itself and runs to the first floor, while a second stairway – added by Mesmakher in around 1882 – curves up to the left and leads to the east wing. The stairs and the massive staircase balustrades are in white marble, the balustrades heavily carved into an intricate intertwined motif of the letter "B" (V in the Russian alphabet) and a griffin from the Romanov coat of arms. The lower part of the stairwell is decorated in tinted smooth scagliola, while the upper area has rich mouldings against a grained and gilded plaster background. A wall niche on the lower level originally held an antique gesso Cupid and Psyche, while a marble statue, 'First Whispers of Love' by Professor Vasili Brodsky, stood on the first floor landing. The ceiling is decorated with a painting entitled 'A genius on the banks of the Neva river' painted by Vereshchagin – the subject could possibly be interpreted as a reference to the Grand Duke Vladimir and his palace on the banks of the Neva. An elegantly curved bay window above the half landing and huge mirrors along the side walls provide the stairs with abundant natural light. The Art Nouveau painting on the mirrors was added in 1910 after Vladimir had died.

The private rooms of the Grand Duchess Maria Pavlovna were located on the first floor at the western end. In 1874 Vladimir married the twenty year old daughter of the Grand Duke of Mecklenburg-Schwerin. The palace was completed long before Vladimir married, so he became the first grand duke to bring his bride into an already finished home. Maria Pavlovna was intelligent, well-educated, attractive, devoid of both prejudices and scruples, and refused to convert to the Orthodox Russian Church. She managed to outshine other relatives – even her sister-in-law the Empress – giving lavish fancy dress balls and costly receptions. The Grand Duchess Maria was an accomplished hostess who liked to entertain celebrities. She was a fanatic gambler and not only regularly visited casinos while on her frequent trips abroad, but also installed a roulette wheel in her private rooms. She received divorced people – which no other grand duchess did – and a number of nouveaux riche were admitted to her salon. As a result the real Russian aristocracy tried to avoid it.

Her Antechamber, with its open balcony onto the main courtyard, was once decorated in Pompeian style, but after her marriage she had it altered to a Winter Garden by Mesmakher. The heavy and ornate furniture in this area was

RIGHT: Ceiling painting entitled 'Dawn', by Tony Fèvre, in Maria's Study - a gift from her mother-in-law, the Empress Maria Alexandrovna.

Tony Faivre

TOP: Detail of the Moorish style lamps, in gilded bronze with red and blue decoration.

ABOVE: The folding wooden doors of the Boudoir are divided into panels and decorated with narrow columns and Arabic style arches.

OPPOSITE: Gilded pine mushrabeyeh cover the windows, which originally also had yellow satin hangings.

designed by Shroeter. The Drawing Room, with its wonderful view of the river, was decorated in Louis XVI style. The walls were covered in blue and white patterned silk, the furniture was painted white and covered with blue satin, and a blue carpet with a grey pattern was spread on the floor. The room was later changed to the existing colour scheme.

The Grand Duchess' Study, with its original colour scheme of soft gold tones, must have presented a pleasant contrast to the blues of the Drawing Room. The Louis XVI style furniture in beech was covered in rich satin upholstery. One lintel panel has a beautifully sculptured relief of children playing – representing Science and Art – by Alexander Opekushin. The ceiling painting, set in a heavy gilded frame, is a canvas entitled 'Dawn' by the Frenchman Tony Fèvre and was a gift from the Empress Maria to her daughter-in-law.

After all this classical French decor the Boudoir, with its exotic and colourful Moorish decoration, is a considerable surprise. The walls are covered with an elaborate moulded stucco design of inscriptions from the Koran, highlighted in gold against a background of red and blue. The frieze has further inscriptions from the Koran in both Arabic and Russian. Low soft settees were covered in cashmere, all the furniture was designed by Shroeter. The small tables of stained pear wood, painted in cinnabar and ultramarine and with engraved glass tops, were made by the cabinet maker Kerim, as were the little stools with their tiny cushions. The unusual lanterns on the walls are of gilded bronze. Above the carved white marble fireplace is a portrait of Helen, the youngest child of the family, dressed in Moorish style. She eventually married Prince Nicholas of Greece and became the mother of Marina, the Duchess of Kent.

The Bedroom of the Grand Duchess was decorated in Louis XVI style, with lavender satin upholstery and walls painted with medallions en grisaille. The original furniture has gone, but the painted ceiling, an elaborate frieze and the moulded arch around the former bed alcove still remain.

The suite of ceremonial rooms on the first floor consisted of the Raspberry Parlour, a Family Dining room, the Ballroom, another main Drawing Room and a large Banqueting Hall. The Raspberry Parlour, at the front of the palace, was the main reception room. Its windows look out over the Neva, with a door to the balcony above the main entrance which provides a marvellous view of the Peter and Paul Fortress opposite. The room is decorated in Italian Renaissance style and the rich dark raspberry colour of the upholstery, wallcovering and curtains goes well with the black wood furniture and the black marble fireplace. Nine dozen chairs were commissioned from Italy to fit into this parlour and the main Drawing Room, but are now dispersed throughout the palace. The mag-

nificent chandelier in the centre of the ceiling is of milky white Venetian glass. The room was hung with many pictures – landscapes, seascapes, views of Dutch towns and churches – all paintings of fine quality by well known artists of the day such as Repin, Karl Bryulov, and Makovsky. Most of them are now displayed in the museums of St Petersburg. A painting by Schwabbe of 'Grand Duke Vladimir Hunting a Brown Bear in the outskirts of St Petersburg' still remains. Grand Duke Vladimir was a genuine connoisseur of many forms of art, a passionate collector of icons, and was a painter of considerable talent himself. He was President of the Imperial Academy of Arts from 1876 until his death in 1909, and a benefactor and friend to many Russian artists. Most of the decor and the furniture remaining in this room is believed to be original.

The Family Dining Room, on the far side of the Raspberry Parlour, was in English Gothic style. Stucco work in the room was painted to imitate oak and there was an eyecatching fireplace decorated with motifs from the Middle Ages. This room underwent drastic changes in later years and none of the original decor now remains.

Behind the Family Dining Room in the east wing, the Ballroom is decorated in Louis XV Rococo style with an elaborate music gallery at each end. The ornate moulding of the coved and coffered ceiling includes beautifully sculptured figures of nymphs and cherubs. The three medallion paintings in the ceiling and the wall decoration were all executed by Vereshchagin, using a colour scheme of subdued greyish cream highlighted with gold. The hall was used for New Year and Christmas celebrations and for receptions for officers of the Imperial Guard, as well as for balls.

The Vladimir family was famous for fancy dress balls. One of them, with guests in 16th century costume, took place here in 1883 and was mentioned by Alexander Polovtsov – then Secretary of the State Council – in his diaries: "The Empress was wearing a historically perfect costume of a Tsarina, inspired by a sketch of a Tsarina's dress by Prince Grigory Gagarin – an amazing richness of fabric and precious stones. My wife put on a Russian costume in the fashion of the 11th century, my daughter had a Tartar style costume, I was wearing a costume a la Stolnik (a rank in the 17th century) Potyomkin, a Russian ambassador to England. All the grand dukes were magnificently dressed; the gentlemen's costumes, as a rule, were more historically accurate than the ladies...."

Careful preparations for such a party began long beforehand; in December 1882 Maria ordered books to be delivered from the Art Academy Library with drawings of 17th century boyar costumes. Vladimir's son, Grand Duke Cyril, described a ball in 1900 at his father's palace where all the men were wearing

ABOVE: The distinctive spire of the Peter and Paul Fortress, on the opposite side of the Neva river, can be seen through the window of the Raspberry Parlour.

OPPOSITE: Most of the decor and the furniture remaining in the Raspberry Parlour is believed to date from when Grand Duke Vladimir lived in the palace.

ABOVE: The brightly painted tiles of the stove were specially commissioned at the workshop of Leonard Bonafedes in St Petersburg.

LEFT: Traditional Russian folk elements were used in the design of the Large Banqueting Hall. The paintings on the walls are of ten popular Russian fairytales, interpreted by Vereshchagin in oil on a special rough canvas to make them look like tapestries.

ABOVE: The pierced design of the chandeliers is based on traditional hand made Russian lace from Vologda, a little town between Moscow and St Petersburg. The elaborate hanging chains and the gilded bronze pendants suspended beneath the bottom tier were made by Johann Benz.

Polish costumes of the time of Emperor Napoleon and the ladies dressed in Empire style. This particular fancy ball was such a success that it was repeated in the Hermitage at the request of Tsar Nicholas II.

The main Drawing Room was in those days located between the Ballroom and the large Banqueting Hall. It was designed in Italian Renaissance style, but the architect Maximilian Mesmakher remodelled it in 1882-83 into an English Gothic Library. The palace had three libraries on three different floors, as books brought great pleasure to Vladimir – particularly books on history. Emperor Alexander II had bequeathed his own personal library to his son Vladimir, although in all he had five surviving sons. Unfortunately, immediately after the Bolshevik coup in 1917, almost all the books from the Grand Duke Vladimir Palace were sold off at random by weight. The major part ended up in the Congress Library and the Harvard and Illinois University Libraries in the USA.

At the rear of the main building is another surprising room, the Large Banqueting Hall, which is decorated in an unusual style based on traditional Russian folk elements. The ceiling, panelling, cornice, and borders are all painted in imitation of oak, which makes the room seem stately but rather sombre. The original furniture was in solid oak with embossed leather upholstery. Ten popular Russian fairy tales decorate the walls, interpreted by Vereshchagin in oil on a special rough canvas that makes them look like tapestries. The spaces between the pictures were originally painted blue and decorated with a Russian folk motifs. The frieze under the ceiling displayed Russian proverbs in Cyrillic script, good-humoured suggestions for the feasting guests: "There's no good dinner without a hostess", "Eat bread and salt and tell the truth", "Eat well and live long", "Drink well, but not to oblivion". The unique chandeliers and wall sconces in polished red copper were made specially for the room by the master craftsman Strange. The windows along one wall, which look out onto the main courtyard, had curtains of unbleached linen with Russian silk embroidery. The back wall has a stove with brightly painted tiles, which were specially commissioned at the workshop of Leonard Bonafedes in St Petersburg. The Large Banqueting Hall was not only used for banquets, but also used for the annual "Merry Christmas" kissing ceremony between master and servants which lasted for many hours.

The palace was somewhat altered in 1881-1891 to the plans of Mesmakher, who created new interiors such as the foyer in place of a buffet room near the Family Dining Room, and the Gold Staircase which connects the first floor to the ground floor in the east wing. The kitchen was also removed and replaced with a Small Banqueting Hall. This new Banqueting Hall was decorated with Russian motifs and has a magnificent fireplace. It was intended for gentlemen's 'stag parties', where Grand Duke Vladimir indulged himself in gluttony and drinking among the shady people he was said to surround himself with. Vladimir did not believe in human virtues, and considered almost everybody to be a bit of a rascal; he liked the company of witty, entertaining rascals but could not stand the dull ones. He often intimidated both relatives and strangers with his coarse loud voice, rudeness, and hot temper. The younger grand dukes avoided starting a conversation with him unless they had prepared themselves beforehand to discuss art or the nuances of French food. As General Mossolov wrote: "Vladimir Alexandrovich was an undisputed authority. Nobody ever dared to argue with him, only in a tête-a-tête would the Grand Duke allow anyone to contradict him."

There was no other court in St Petersburg of greater renown and importance than the Vladimirs. Even their servants looked more important than most – Grand Duchess Maria wanted them to look elegant, and in 1874 new summer

ABOVE LEFT: Detail of the elaborate caryatids and cherubs around ceiling of the Ballroom.

ABOVE RIGHT: The magnificent fireplace in the Small Banqueting Hall, which was installed in place of the former Kitchen by Mesmakher.

outfits were tailored in scarlet with a sword, mace and a square shaped hat. In the streets Vladimir's carriages, emblazoned with his coat of arms and with coachmen and footmen dressed in scarlet or in the green raccoon trimmed winter uniforms, always drew the attention of passers by.

A few times Vladimir became the heir presumptive and the alluring and enticing Russian Crown came within his grasp, but he never became emperor. Much later in 1924 his son the Grand Duke Cyril, as senior in succession in the Romanov family in exile, proclaimed himself Emperor of all the Russias. This caused protests and the rejection of his claim by the Dowager Empress Maria Feodorovna and many emigrés all over Europe. Vladimir's grandson, Grand Duke Vladimir Cyrillovich, sensibly did not aspire to the title of Emperor although he retained the title of Head of the Imperial family. Vladimir Cyrillovich had no son, and upon his death in 1992 the male seniority of the Vladimirovich in the Romanov dynasty came to an end.

After 1917 the Grand Duke Vladimir Palace was much more fortunate than

ABOVE: The Gold Staircase in the east wing, installed in 1881-91 by Mesmakher.

TOP RIGHT: Detail of the elaborate metalwork of the Gold Staircase.

ABOVE RIGHT: Two cherubs support a cartouche with an elaborate monogram of the intertwined letters "B" (V in the Russian alphabet), "M" and "P" (R in the Russian alphabet) - for Vladimir, Maria and Romanov.

other palaces, many of which were robbed, mistreated, and demolished. As the Scientists' Club, money has been available to maintain the building in good shape. Almost all the contents are still intact, although some furniture has been moved from room to room and a certain amount of refurbishment work has been done. Originally built for a patron of the arts, the palace is now dedicated to the scientists of St Petersburg – art and science have come together in one fascinating building.

CHAPTER
NINE

The Shuvalov Palace

THE SHUVALOV PALACE was never a Romanov property, yet it can be rated as part of their legacy. Imperial Russia under the Romanovs reached its zenith of artistic endeavour and culture and the beautiful city of St Petersburg, having been founded by a Romanov, grew and developed under their rule. The many splendid palaces of the Imperial family undoubtedly give St Petersburg and its surrounding area a unique glory, but the Russian aristocracy also built palaces there even before the city become established as the new centre of power. In the many-textured society of the period they had the time, money and intellect to collect, create and appreciate beauty and their wonderful palaces are almost as sumptuous as those of the Romanovs.

The Shuvalov Palace was not in fact built by a Shuvalov. The original building on the fashionable right bank of the Fontanka river, in the centre of St Petersburg itself, was a small mansion built by Countess Vorontsova in 1790. Soon afterwards the building was purchased by the Naryshkins, who were the wealthiest aristocrats in St Petersburg and relations of the Imperial family – in 1671 the widowed Tsar Alexis Mikhailovich had married Natalia Kirillovna Naryshkina and their son, Peter the Great, was the founder of St Petersburg.

The house was intended as a wedding gift for Dimitri Naryshkin who in 1795 married Maria Chetvertynsky, the beautiful daughter of a Polish count. The marriage was not a success, as Maria's improbable, striking beauty quickly attracted the attention of Emperor Alexander I. Their passionate liaison was common knowledge, and Dimitri acquired an unenviable reputation as a cuckold while Maria was known as the uncrowned Russian queen. The affair lasted until 1814, but they remained friends after it was over. Maria had six children, but her husband Dimitri considered only Marina to be his child; Alexander I provided for the three surviving children.

All this was in the future, however, and for the moment the house was enlarged and refurbished for the newly-weds. The eminent architect Giacomo Quarenghi was commissioned to re-design the building, and he also created a new façade by adding a portico with eight columns and a pediment. This was a feature that was particularly well liked by the NeoClassicists in St Petersburg, and thus the façade of the palace now slightly resembled the fronts of the Smolny and Catherine Institutes, the latter located right across the river.

In 1822-23, Count Dimitri enlarged the palace again by building on the Colonnade Hall and a hall to be used as a museum. The architect for this work is not known, but he is believed to have been one of the associates of Carlo Rossi. Dimitri invited the best decorators of the period – artists such as Giovanni Scotti – to work on the rooms.

LEFT: Ceiling detail of the Vestibule dome, showing the elaborate moulded decoration. Each of the small caryatids at the base of the dome holds a different symbol of the arts.

RIGHT: The imposing Vestibule has a gallery at first floor level with a highly ornate and decorative wrought iron balustrade designed by Corsini.

Count Dimitri was a true aristocrat in both appearance and manner; he was Master of the Imperial Hunt and was famous for his lavish balls, receptions, and concerts. He owned 25,000 serfs, many of whom were very talented singers and musicians who performed at his concerts. His sumptuous and extravagant lifestyle came to an abrupt end in awful financial embarrassment, and his disloyal wife managed to have him put away.

In 1838 the palace passed to Dimitri's nephew, Count Lev Alexandrovich Naryshkin. Lev Alexandrovich was lazy, careless, inconsistent and a terrible womanizer. His wife Olga did not get on with him at all and consequently had love affairs of her own. No changes were made during the eight years they owned the palace, as everything came to a standstill because of the poor relations between them. In 1846 Lev's only child, Sophie, married Count Peter Shuvalov and the palace was part of her dowry. Count Shuvalov was Marshal of the Nobility in the St Petersburg region under the reign of Alexander II. The Shuvalovs were also incredibly wealthy and owned platinum mines in the Urals.

The young couple began immediate alterations to arrange their home according to their own tastes and in the latest style. The building was greatly

PREVIOUS PAGE: The Shuvalov Palace stands on the banks of the Fontanka river in the centre of St Petersburg. The huge oriel window in the centre was added by Nicholas Yefimov in the mid 19th century.

expanded and the façade was altered to its present design by the architect Nicholas Yefimov (1799-1851). He installed a larger Vestibule, in place of the gates and the small entrance hall, and gave a Renaissance outlook to the main front with high windows to both storeys and an intricate frieze of niched cherubs alternating with the heads of young girls. The columns and portico were removed leaving a flat façade, but the monotony was broken by Corinthian half-fluted pilasters on the first floor and a huge oriel window in the centre. The house was painted in pale grey-green, with the ornamentation picked out in white.

The palace is a huge hollow square in shape, with an inner courtyard providing light to the rooms which face inwards. These were used as private apartments – bedrooms, boudoir, children's rooms, and family dining room. The interior was redesigned by the architect Bernard Simon (1816-1900) in the Eclectic fashion of the mid-19th century, each room echoing a different historical style.

The main entrance leads into the imposing Vestibule, which occupies the entire width of the building on the ground floor between the front façade and the central courtyard. The grand sweep of the main staircase begins in the Vestibule with a single wide flight of stairs leading to a half landing, from which two stairways ascend to the first floor gallery. The highly ornate and decorative wrought iron balustrade to the staircase and gallery makes an effective contrast to the plain and simple white walls. The metalwork was designed by the artist Corsini who, in 1837, also designed the metalwork railings for the Count Sheremetev Palace, directly opposite across the Fontanka river.

The gallery runs round the stairwell at first floor level and has twelve columns of scagliola supporting a wide and ornate frieze. On the wall behind each column is a matching pilaster, and the lintels running between the two divide the ceiling above the gallery into a series of peculiar miniature vaults in a rather Gothic style. The moulded stucco design features medieval bearded characters wearing berets.

The massive dome has a central glass cupola, surrounded with four lions' masks set between decorative mouldings in relief. The dome rests on the frieze at eight points, each point features a small caryatid holding a symbol of the arts – a musical instrument, a book, an easel. In each corner is an elaborate pendant, from which hangs a gilded bronze chandelier decorated with four winged dragons. Two NeoClassical marble statues of young men, made in France, miraculously still stand in the same niches at the top of the stairs as in the Naryshkins' day.

ABOVE: Detail of the frieze, around the Colonnade Hall, with its delicate moulded motifs in white and gold set against a beige background. The paintings around the ceiling are of mythological scenes.

LEFT: The ceiling of the Colonnade Hall was painted by Giovanni Scotti. Although the ceiling is perfectly flat, the design of the border makes it appear to have a shallow cove.

BELOW: The bas-relief panels between the Corinthian columns feature episodes from the Trojan War. They are nearly two metres high and replace the original upper windows.

The main ceremonial rooms run across the front of the palace, overlooking the Fontanka river. At the far north end is the Colonnade Hall, or Concert Hall, which is believed to have been originally conceived by Quarenghi in two tiers. Quarenghi died in 1817 so the work was finally carried out in 1822-23 by someone else, who endowed the room with a strong Empire style. The engaged columns of beige scagliola have Corinthian capitals with details picked out in gold. Set between them at high level are panels nearly two metres high with bas-reliefs of episodes from the Trojan War. These panels replace the original upper windows, which were done away with during reconstruction work in later years. Above the columns is a frieze with delicate moulded motifs in white, picked out in gold and set against a beige background. Only three tones were used in the entire colour scheme – white, beige and gold.

The ceiling was elaborately painted by Giovanni Scotti en grisaille. The two larger paintings of the ceiling border are 'Rape of the Sabine women' and 'Bacchanalia', the smaller paintings are mythological scenes. The border paintings are set between painted caryatids, while a pair of winged lions guards each corner of the ceiling. The design of the border makes the ceiling appear to have

ABOVE: Ornate carving in dark polished walnut, with decorative details picked out in bright gold, gives the fireplace and doors a rich opulence.

ABOVE RIGHT: Detail of the unusual 'barley-twist' half pillars in polished walnut, topped with gilded cherubs.

LEFT: The Gold Drawing Room is designed in a mixture of the styles common in the time of Nicholas I. Only three colours are used in the room: gold, white and the rich brown of dark polished walnut.

a shallow cove, although in fact it is perfectly flat. The two paintings in the centre of the ceiling are 'Gods on Olympus' and 'Marriage of Cupid and Psyche'. A fine Italian statue of Apollo, a copy of an antique original, was placed opposite the entrance for 125 years but has now vanished.

The Colonnade Hall was famous for its excellent acoustics and charity concerts often took place there. Dimitri Naryshkin held a fancy dress ball here, each year, with guests in the costumes of former eras. Much later other less discerning owners turned the hall into a storage area and also used it to play tennis in. The last owner, Elizaveta V. Shuvalova who lived at the palace until 1917, revived its artistic glory. The great theatrical performances were resumed and a permanent stage and orchestra box were installed.

In 1914 the Shuvalovs donated their palace as a hospital and the Colonnade

BELOW: The white marble fireplace in the Blue Drawing Room is heavily carved into a lavish design of cherubs, flower garlands, scrolls and acanthus leaves.

ABOVE: Detail of the fireplace carving.

OPPOSITE: The Blue Drawing Room, with its lighthearted Rococo decoration and bright colour scheme of blue, white and gold, is in strong contrast to the darker and more sombre rooms on either side.

ABOVE: The deep frieze at high level is moulded into an elaborate pattern of interlocking circles and stylized shells, the shapes highlighted in gold against the white background.

Hall served as a ward for wounded officers. In 1941, during the siege of Leningrad, a bomb exploded in the hall causing a terrible fire which also destroyed the three authentic gilt bronze chandeliers which had been hanging from the ceiling since the time of Emperor Alexander I. The decoration of the room has now been restored and it is used as a lecture theatre.

To the south of the Colonnade Hall is the Gold Drawing Room, which was formerly the Large Dining Room. The decor is a typical mixture of styles common in the time of Nicholas I: Baroque, Gothic, and Classical. Again only three colours are used in the colour scheme – gold, dark brown polished walnut and white. The walls are covered in golden yellow silk damask, with matching fabric pelmets to doors and windows. The original upholstery would have been similar. Below the dado is dark tinted panelling, and the exquisite boldly carved doors are in polished walnut. The window and door portals have extremely unusual 'barley-twist' half-pillars in dark wood topped with gilded cherubs, which support heavily ornate lintels.

The deep frieze around the room features elaborate mouldings of knights and damsels in medieval costume, enhanced with gold detailing. The vaulted ceiling is divided into five separate areas by arches which spring from corbels on the

LEFT: Detail of the barrel vaulted ceiling designed by Bernard Simon in the Red Drawing Room. The two panels on either side of the centre in the foreground show the Naryshkin coat of arms in moulded stucco.

RIGHT: The Red Drawing Room has a distinct Renaissance feel. The "door" on the left hand side of the picture is in fact a enormous mirror, with the same architraves, lintels and pelmets as the real doors.

walls. The arches have an open window on each side in which stands the rampant figure of a lion with a golden mane and tail. The ceiling panels are heavily moulded in white stucco, picked out in gold. The Naryshkin coat-of-arms, a gold eagle against a bright red and blue background, is set in the ceiling at one end of the room. The room originally contained artworks such as a Thomire bronze, twelve paintings by Western masters, and a marble relief of the school of Antonio Rossellino, but these are now displayed in various museums in St Petersburg.

The unexpected exuberance of the Blue Drawing Room, in the centre of the ceremonial suite above the main entrance, is due to its bright colour scheme of blue, white and gold and lighthearted Rococo decoration. This is the largest room in the suite and its decor is in strong contrast to the darker and more sombre rooms on either side.

The walls above the dado are upholstered in rich blue brocade and were originally hung with portraits of the Naryshkin-Shuvalov family and their relations, painted by eminent Western and Russian portrait painters such as Jean-Baptiste Greuze, Johann von Lampi, Feodor Rokotov, Dimitri Levitsky, Karl Bryulov, François Boucher, Vladimir Hau, Franz Winterhalter, and Christina Robertson. Below the dado the walls are panelled in wood, painted white with

the mouldings picked out in gold. The doors and architraves are also white with gold detailing. The extremely deep frieze at high level has a highly elaborate moulded stucco design of interlocking circles and stylized shells, the shapes highlighted in gold against the white background. The four oval medallions set in the frieze along each side show mythological scenes, the four round medallion portraits at each end are purely decorative.

The cornice design and the delicate ceiling mouldings are again picked out in gold against a white background. In the centre of the ceiling is a huge moulded stucco Rococo rosette from which hangs an exquisite gilt bronze chandelier decorated with the Naryshkin coat of arms.

Two arches divide the room into three sections. The four fluted half-columns which support the arches have unusual capitals with gilded caryatids at each corner, while halfway up each column is a heavily ornate gilt bronze sconce. The room is flooded with light from five enormous windows which overlook the river. On either side of the central window gold Rococo consoles are decorated with cherubs and lions, above them enormous mirrors in heavy gold frames almost reach up to the level of the frieze.

The fireplace of white marble is intricately carved into a lavish design of cherubs, flower garlands, scrolls, latticework and acanthus leaves. The same white marble is used for the window cills and the tops of the consoles. The original furniture was in gold with blue plush upholstery, but it vanished long ago.

The final room at the extreme south end of the suite is the Red Drawing Room, which was also called the Naryshkinskaya (Naryshkin Room). This room has a distinct Renaissance feel, with its barrel vaulted ceiling, red brocade walls and dark polished walnut woodwork. Simon designed the ceiling with moulded ribs, running across and lengthways, which divide it up into panels. Six of the panels contain the Naryshkin coat of arms in moulded stucco, highlighted in gold. At each point where the ribs cross there is a tiny gold boss, with a design of animals at the hunt. Where the main ribs spring from the walls there is a decorative gilded stucco bracket shaped as a huge bat.

The walls above the low dado rail are covered in rich red brocade, while below the dado they are panelled in dark wood. The doors are in highly polished dark walnut, with heavily ornate lintels and red brocade pelmets. Opposite the two doors in the north wall are two enormous mirrors, with the same architraves, lintels and pelmets, which give the room a symmetrical appearance. The two windows which overlook the Fontanka are again in dark polished walnut, with the same lintel and pelmet as the doors. Between them is another enormous mirror, above which is a painting of a mythological scene. The rich

RIGHT: The small Gothic style Knights' Hall was originally the library, lined with shelves containing many thousands of books. These all vanished, along with many of the artworks in the palace, after the revolution of 1917.

RIGHT: Detail of the frieze, which shows scenes of a medieval tournament: knights preparing for the contest, jousting, and receiving favours from a lady.

colour of the brocade, the dark shine of the wood and the glow of the gold detailing make this whole room look magnificently opulent.

The small Knights' Hall, which is in the south wing, was designed in Gothic style. The ceiling is vaulted and finished in simple plain white plaster. The walls at high level have a deep moulded frieze with detailed scenes of a medieval tournament: knights preparing for the contest, jousting, and receiving favours from a lady. Count Peter Shuvalov used this room as his library and it was originally lined with shelves containing many thousands of books.

Before 1917 the palace was full of valuable artwork. There were over 200 paintings, precious tapestries, 15th and 16th century faience from Italy, 16th century French faience by Bernard Palissy, Limoges enamels, silver of all periods, Greek ceramics, porcelain and beautiful glassware. During World War I the Shuvalov family hid most of their silverware, bronze and paintings under the floorboards – as did many of the aristocratic families in St Petersburg – where it was later discovered by the Bolsheviks. In 1919-23 a museum of the 'nobleman's lifestyle' was opened in 17 rooms of the Shuvalov Palace, to display some of this rich hoard. Although it is no longer in the palace, part of this valuable and varied artistic collection can now be seen at the Hermitage.

From 1923-27 the Shuvalov Palace housed The Press Centre, with some rooms used as communal flats and private apartments, and in 1930 it became the Centre of Science-technical Engineering. Apart from the bomb in the Colonnade Hall, the building was not greatly damaged during the siege of Leningrad. After the Second World War it was assigned to accommodate the local Peace Committee and Friendship societies, who still occupy the building.

Index

Numbers in italics refer to captions and page numbers of illustrations. Buildings are in or around St Petersburg unless stated otherwise